FOOD TO GROW ON

GIVE YOUR KIDS A HEALTHY START IN LIFE

SUSAN MENDELSON AND RENA MENDELSON, M.S., D.Sc.

A Today's Parent Book

HarperPerennial

HarperCollins*PublishersLtd*

First Edition

Canadian Cataloguing in Publication Data

Mendelson, Susan and Rena
Food to grow on

(A Today's Parent book)
HarperPerennial ed.
Includes index.
ISBN 0-00-638019-0

1. Children – Nutrition.   2. Cookery.   I. Mendelson, Susan, 1952-   .
II. Title.   III. Series.

RJ206.M45 1993   641.5'6   C93-094624-3

94 95 96 97 98 99 ❖ EB 10 9 8 7 6 5 4 3 2 1

Printed in the United States

Cover Design: Andrew Smith

Page Design and Composition: Joseph Gisini, Andrew Smith Graphics, Inc.

Illustrations: Susan Todd

For our mother, Roz.
With love and admiration.

Table of Contents

PART ONE
BEFORE THE BEGINNING

PART TWO
....
INFANCY

PART THREE

CHILDHOOD

Foreword

On first glance, one might think that this is a cookbook with some nutritional rules for kids, or a nutritional rule book with some recipes. It is neither. It is a practical book, written by two people who have their own kids, have an excellent formal background in the principles of nutrition, and love to eat.

In my practice as a pediatric clinical nutritionist, I continue to be amazed that something as intuitive as feeding one's infant or child is so often seen by parents as mysterious and daunting. The result is parents who feel frustrated and guilty, and children who are over- or underweight and, as important, do not enjoy the process of eating. Susan and Rena Mendelson have recognized that the world of feeding one's offspring, literally from the moment of conception, is full of rules about what to eat, how to feed your child, how many helpings of this, and how many glasses of that. These rules, created by government officials and scientists, have taken the fun out of eating for many people, young and old. Susan and Rena's book not only takes the mystery out of meeting nutrient needs, but conveys the sense that eating can and should be fun. Their book clearly proclaims that getting kids to enjoy mealtimes involves much more than just the food that is presented to them.

The skills and experience of these two sisters is a wonderful combination. Rena has years of experience as a nutrition educator at Ryerson Polytechnic University and Susan as a cook and caterer. And, most important, these two women have intuitive smarts about food and behaviour. They recognize and address the complex relationship between the feeder and the individuals being fed. Food is much more than a combination of nutrients. It is often a reward and sometimes a punishment. It can be a source of pleasure and even a source of tension. This book recognizes the complexity of the behavioural components of eating and food, and incorporates this recognition both in the suggestions for getting kids and pregnant women to eat right and in the recipes.

I cannot count the number of times I have told parents to feed kids only according to their appetite rather than insist that they clean their plates, only to be met with a blank stare of disbelief and disdain. Rena and Susan write, "Feed your child to meet her particular appetite; that is, do not force feed her, but try to ensure that she gets enough calories to keep healthy. Of course this is easier said than done. I have encouraged each of my children to take just one more bite only to have them throw up on their plate after eating beyond their appetite. You really shouldn't mess with Mother Nature." By writing in a style that is personal, including anecdotes about their own kids and family, and extremely practical, they have managed to include the rules, but in a way that makes the reader forget they are rules.

Congratulations to Susan and Rena Mendelson, who have written a book that will be used by parents for years and years. This book truly is the children's version of Jane Brody's lifetime guide to good eating.

STANLEY ZLOTKIN, MD, PhD, FRCP(C)
DIVISION OF CLINICAL NUTRITION
THE HOSPITAL FOR SICK CHILDREN

Why We Wrote This Book

The foods we ate as children are a far cry from the recipes in this book. With four picky eaters to feed and a strong personal preference for chocolate bars and coffee, our mother did not inspire us to think about nutrition. We consider ourselves lucky that our Home Economics courses had generous budgets and used interesting recipes.

People often ask how three of us ended up with an interest in food. (Our sister Lynn wrote the runaway bestseller *Chicken! Chicken! Chicken!*) The truth is that our Grandma Faye inspired each of us to cater elaborate meals. We can't remember a single one of hers that didn't have at least four or five courses—and that includes breakfast. Our father and our brother, Fred, were the only ones who ate everything she made. She was famous in Quebec City for her fabulous fare. It's hard to figure out why our mother was placed on feeding supplements to keep up her weight.

While Rena went off to pursue a doctorate in nutrition at Harvard, Susan was selling cheesecake and Nanaimo bars. Eventually our interests began to merge as the nutritionist began to appreciate the importance of taste and the caterer began to appreciate the importance of nutrition. We have been fascinated with the responses of our own children to various foods and finally decided to merge our interests and talents into a single project to help other parents through the confusing and challenging stages of raising healthy children.

SUSAN MENDELSON AND RENA MENDELSON

PART ONE

BEFORE THE BEGINNING

NUTRITION IS AN IMPORTANT PART OF HEALTH PROMOtion at every stage of the lifespan, but most people would agree that it deserves special consideration during the earliest stage of life. For this reason, no one pays more attention to nutrition than expectant and new parents. From this chapter you will learn about nutritional needs and concerns not only during pregnancy but also during the time leading up to it. Because, believe it or not, the impact of nutrition and health on pregnancy begins before conception. Along with information about the key nutrition issues, we have provided some exciting and innovative recipes to help you put this information to use.

Preconceptional Nutrition

If you're considering an addition to your family, you should be concerned about nutrition and health before conception and during pregnancy. You'll have questions about both yourself and your baby, from how much weight to gain to how much alcohol or coffee is safe to drink.

Some mothers tell themselves, "I will change my eating habits when I know I am pregnant." This is usually applied to a whole set of health behaviours such as smoking, alcohol consumption, exercise, and nutrition. For this reason, everyone in your family should anticipate the pregnancy well ahead of conception and establish good eating and health practices. These positive lifestyle choices will help you provide a healthy environment for the protection and nourishment of your developing baby.

It is tough to make so many sudden changes to your lifestyle. Perhaps this is why some popular prenatal programs encourage women to apply even before they have conceived. These programs prepare parents for pregnancy both physically and emotionally. It makes sense to prepare ahead because most people never can tell when the critical moment of conception has taken place, marking the beginning of a new life. In fact, pregnancy may not be confirmed until some time after major development has already occurred.

Concerns about adequate growth before pregnancy used to be restricted to countries in which poverty is a major concern. However, North American dieting trends of the last two decades may have created a group of child-bearing women who have chosen to starve themselves for the sake of a fashionable look. The early dieting and food restrictions that young women endure through chronic dieting, anorexia nervosa, or bulimia may influence future generations by reducing the nutritional status of potentially healthy women to that of women who live in poverty. In fact, if early dieting experiences are prolonged, they can lead to fertility problems such as irregular menstrual cycles, cessation of menstruation (amenorrhea), or problems of conception. A recent survey of women attending a fertility clinic in Toronto revealed that more than half could be classified as having an eating disorder.

More and more attention is being paid to the health of women who may become pregnant. This applies to warnings about workplace hazards, smoking, and drinking. The Food and

Drug Administration in Washington recently advised all women who might become pregnant to increase their intake of the vitamin folic acid (also known as folate) in order to prevent neural tube defects. They went so far as to say that a daily vitamin supplement was recommended for women who could not eat enough of the natural sources (dark green vegetables and beans). This is an unprecedented move for this organization and represents the first time that a nutrient supplement has been recommended specifically for women who might become pregnant.

The Effect of Birth Control Methods on Nutrition in Pregancy

It comes as a surprise to many that during the first trimester of pregnancy (the first twelve to fourteen weeks), the nourishment of the fetus will depend almost exclusively on the nutrients stored in the lining of the mother's uterus. Those nutrients were left there at least six months before conception. But it's never too late to change your diet, even after the pregnancy test comes back positive.

Various factors will have affected these nutritional stores. Obviously, diet is a major contributor. But body stores can also be influenced by the chronic use of drugs such as oral contraceptives or by birth control devices such as the IUD. Therefore, if you are planning a pregnancy, you should consider the effect of various types of birth control methods on your nutritional status. For example, if you have used an intrauterine device (IUD), you may have lost large amounts of blood during menstruation and may be slightly anemic. (In fact, most women are so low in iron stores that iron supplements are recommended as a routine for all pregnant women after the first trimester.) Or if you have been taking oral contraceptives for several years, you may have good iron stores but low stores of the B vitamins, such as folate, vitamin B_{12}, and vitamin B_6. (At one time, a clever vitamin manufacturer came up with the "pill pill," a vitamin supplement designed for women on the pill.)

The good news for women on the pill is that menstrual blood losses are lower with the pill and iron deficiency is less likely. In either case, it is probably a good idea to stop using IUDs or the pill at least six months before conceiving in order to increase your body's nutritional stores. Mechanical devices such as diaphragms or condoms and spermicidal jellies have no known effect on the nutritional stores for pregnancy.

Alcohol

Alcohol is the most widely used and abused drug in the world. If you tend to drink heavily, try to eliminate alcohol from your diet completely for a good six months before becoming pregnant.

In the early 1970s, a group of pediatricians in Seattle noticed that babies born to alcoholic women had similar facial features and similar medical problems. The facial features included narrow eye slits which gave the appearance of a wide bridge across the nose. In addition, the babies did not grow at normal rates nor develop mentally beyond a certain level. The mental problems ranged from minor learning disabilities to profound mental disorders. Some of the children had heart problems and abnormal bone development. The pediatricians used the name Fetal Alcohol Syndrome to describe the problem and began to look more closely at the causes. Before that time, there were no rigid alcohol restrictions imposed on women. Alcohol was actually prescribed to prevent premature labour.

The discovery of Fetal Alcohol Syndrome caused a flurry of research activity to find out how widespread the problem might be, how much alcohol was safe to drink during pregnancy, and what could be done for children with the syndrome. Unfortunately, it appears that the damage is permanent. For this reason, some women have been charged with child abuse if they drank excessively during pregnancy. Some have even been denied access to their babies after birth. Although Fetal Alcohol Syndrome appears to be more widespread than originally anticipated, it is unlikely to affect babies whose mothers have had only a few drinks during pregnancy.

It is worth warning women to restrict their alcohol intake if they are considering pregnancy. For this reason, the federal government requires all manufacturers to place warning labels on alcoholic beverages. Moreover, women who consume one to two drinks of alcohol a day during the first and second trimesters have a higher rate of miscarriages. Research has also shown that alcoholic women who stop drinking immediately upon becoming pregnant are more likely to have underweight babies with medical problems, although these problems are greatly reduced compared to those who continue drinking. The best advice is to eliminate alcohol completely before pregnancy, although the occasional drink is unlikely to prove harmful.

Smoking

During recent years, smoking has been blamed for a number of early childhood problems. Mothers who smoke have babies who are significantly smaller than those of non-smokers, and recent quitters have babies who are only slightly underweight. The reason that we worry about birth weight is that babies who are smaller than 5 lbs (3500 g) are at risk for a variety of health problems. One way of reducing these risks is to ensure healthy pregnancies and healthy birth weights. Recently, smoking by mothers has been associated with sudden infant death syndrome (SIDS).

Women who return to smoking after the birth of the baby and fathers who smoke may also cause further problems through second-hand smoke. These include long-term respiratory problems as well as poor growth. Every member of the family should be aware of the need for lifestyle changes in anticipation of a new arrival. It's never too late to quit smoking. A smoke-free home will provide a healthier environment for your baby.

Weight Gain During Pregnancy

An overwhelming concern for those women who have struggled to keep their weights fashionably low is weight gain during pregnancy. How much is enough? How much is too much?

The recommendations regarding weight gain have changed dramatically over the last thirty years. Today's grandmothers remember being told to gain no more than 10 to 15 pounds and many look upon their daughters and daughters-in-law with horror as they gain 30 pounds or more. In the past, those recommendations were intended to keep the baby's weight low so that delivery would be easier. In reality, this older generation lost weight during pregnancy and left the hospital weighing much less than before pregnancy. No wonder these women spent weeks in the hospital. They must have been weakened by the whole experience.

Since that time scientists have come to recognize that the weight gained during pregnancy is essential to meet the needs of the growing infant and the placenta, as well as to maintain the mother's nutritional stores in preparation for breastfeeding.

Furthermore, we have come to realize the risks of low birth weight. We now know that it can be dangerous to produce a small baby.

Today's recommendations for weight gain suggest that women who enter pregnancy with a normal healthy weight should gain 25 to 35 lbs (11 to 15 kg) during pregnancy. A normal healthy weight is defined in a number of ways, one of which is through the Body Mass Index (BMI). By marking your weight and height on the chart and drawing a line through the two points, you can get a reading for your own BMI. If the reading falls within the range of 20 to 25, you are considered a "healthy weight." Women who begin pregnancy with a low BMI (less than 19.8)

Body Mass Index

A — HEIGHT (m) (ft. in.)

B — WEIGHT (kg) (lb.)

C — BMI (kg/m²)

HOW TO FIND YOUR BMI – IT'S EASY

1. Mark an X at your height on line A.
2. Mark an X at your weight on line B.
3. Take a ruler and join the two X's.
4. To find your BMI, extend the line to line C.

FOR EXAMPLE:

- If Michael is 1.80 m (5'11") and weighs 85 kg (188 lbs), his BMI is about 26.
- If Irene is 1.60 m (5'4") and weighs 60 kg (132 lbs), her BMI is about 23.

If you fall below 20 or above 27 on the BMI range...

It's time to reduce your chance of developing health problems. The first and most important thing is to determine why you are not within the healthy weight range and to seek the assistance of your dietitian nutritionist and physician.

Under 20: A BMI under 20 may be associated with health problems for some individuals. It may be a good idea to consult a dietitian and physician for advice.

20–25: This zone is associated with the lowest risk of illness for most people. This is the range you want to stay in.

25–27: A BMI over 25 may be associated with health problems for some people. Caution is suggested if your BMI is in this zone.

Over 27: A BMI over 27 is associated with increased risk of health problems such as heart disease, high blood pressure and diabetes. It may a good idea to consult a dietitian and physician for advice.

Source: Expert Group on Weight Standards, Health and Welfare Canada are encouraged to gain 28 to 40 lbs (13 to 18 kg). On the other hand, women who enter pregnancy with a body mass index of greater than 26 are advised to gain 15 to 25 lbs (7 to 11 kg). Women who are expecting twins are advised to gain 35 to 45 lbs (16 to 20 kg).

The pattern of weight gain is just as important as the total amount gained. During the first trimester, weight gain should only be in the range of two to four pounds. From the second trimester until delivery, the expectant mother should gain approximately one pound (0.45 kg) a week. These numbers should only be used as a guideline. In order to gain this amount of weight and to meet the high nutrient requirements, experts recommend that women rely on a variety of good-quality foods, eat to satisfy their appetites, and get moderate amounts of exercise.

Most women wonder how many calories it takes to gain this much weight. The total amount of energy required during pregnancy is estimated to use up an extra 300 calories per day or thereabouts. That's about one extra glass of 2 percent milk and one piece of buttered toast each day. Not much at all when you need to gain 30 pounds in nine months! The truth is that it is probably not quite so simple. The specific amount of energy required for women during pregnancy will depend on a whole set of factors including how much energy is spent on activities during this time.

It is important to think about weight before your pregnancy. For example, women who are obese or extremely overweight might be wise to watch their dietary intake to ensure that they are not eating excessive fats and calories for several months before conception. Pregnancy is not the time for dieting or food restriction. Likewise, women who are significantly underweight should pay attention to their diets to ensure that they enter pregnancy at an optimally healthy weight.

Appetite

As we are too well aware, some women experience significant vomiting and nausea which may lead to poor eating during the early stages of pregnancy. For most women, the discomfort lasts a few weeks only, but for others it can last much longer.

Once the early stages of pregnancy have passed, a new set of questions arise concerning appetite and weight gain. Now is the time to plan a "nutrient-dense" diet. This includes foods that have a high nutrient-calorie ratio. Remember, you are not really eating for two but rather for one and a bit. Some useful advice to keep you from overeating is to "eat to appetite." This means staying in touch with your body's true feelings of hunger and satiety. In other words, there is no reason to deny yourself food when you are truly hungry, but there is no need to overeat to gain the recommended weight. Besides, much of the weight gain is under the control of those hormones that take over during pregnancy. You may find that during the latter half of pregnancy your activities are reduced because you are uncomfortable and tire more easily. This will mean that you are using less energy and therefore need fewer calories for weight gain.

The weight gained during pregnancy will be lost some time after delivery. This generally holds true for women who have never had a so-called "weight problem." Unfortunately, the weight loss is not as rapid as most women would like and some patience is required. If you breastfeed, you will probably lose the weight gradually and without much effort as you breastfeed. This is because breastfeeding is an extremely energy-demanding activity and helps to burn off calories laid down during pregnancy. If you have a history of chronic dieting (the yo-yo syndrome), losing weight after pregnancy can be a continuation of your earlier battles. For some women, it becomes increasingly difficult with each pregnancy. The best advice is to prepare for the situation and come up with a specific plan to deal with it when the time comes. Seek the help of a dietitian for this problem; don't take it on by yourself or with the advice of well-meaning friends.

Coping with Nausea and Vomiting

Women who experience extreme nausea and vomiting may be hospitalized to ensure they are getting adequate fluids and nutrients to keep them from becoming dehydrated. If you enter pregnancy with healthy nutritional stores in your body, you will be able to provide yourself and your baby with adequate nutrition even if you have a short period of poor eating or vomiting. But for most women who experience an average amount of discomfort, there are a few tips on coping with this unpleasantness. Some women find it helpful to eat a dry cracker before getting out of bed. Eating crackers between meals can also be helpful.

For many women the nausea and vomiting of pregnancy may pass within the first trimester. For others it may extend all the way through to the point of delivery. Small frequent meals may help to ensure comfort.

Another useful treatment is the use of frozen juice pops when nausea threatens. The cooling effect has its own merits and the fruit sugar helps to bring back blood sugar levels to a comfortable zone. Look for this recipe in the recipe section on page 273.

Nutrients of Special Concern During Pregnancy

Throughout pregnancy special attention needs to be paid to specific nutrients which play an important role in the development of the fetus and in the protection of the mother.

Calcium

Think of calcium as an expensive resource which can be deposited or withdrawn from your body's bank account. It is the most important mineral for the development of your baby's bones and teeth as well as the maintenance of your own bone mass. Pregnancy and breastfeeding both create very high demands for calcium because of the tremendous deposits required for a baby's development. These demands are made during pregnancy when the fetus is developing and growing; they are also made when the mother is manufacturing breast milk.

Although calcium is the most abundant mineral in the body, it is found in only a small number of foods. If your diet is too low in these foods, calcium is taken directly from your bones to supply it to the baby during pregnancy and to the milk during breastfeeding. Getting enough calcium from the diet becomes a double challenge for a woman who is less than 25 years old because her own bone mass is still increasing. Mothers who have several children in quick succession and provide them all with breast milk also run the risk of diminished bone mass if they do not sustain a very high calcium intake during this period of child-bearing. If they can't balance the calcium budget, women may be at high risk for calcium bankruptcy (in the form of osteoporosis) in later life.

Calcium is important not only for the development of bones and teeth, but also for muscles and their ability to contract. For example, the smooth muscle of the uterus and the lining of the arteries both rely on calcium for normal function. At one time women were instructed to take calcium to reduce leg cramps, but recent studies have shown that this is not necessary. Other studies have demonstrated that taking 1000-2000 mg of calcium per day may reduce blood pressure for pregnant women and lower the number of cases of high blood pressure brought on by pregnancy. Some (but not all) studies have suggested that there are great benefits from calcium supplements. In one experiment, the use of calcium supplements seemed to reduce the number of premature deliveries and the number of low-birth-weight babies. It is important to point out, however, that pregnancy-induced hypertension (high blood pressure), premature deliveries, and low-birth-weight babies are not caused by a deficiency of calcium alone.

Getting enough calcium during pregnancy may seem challenging, but is as simple as getting at least four servings of dairy products a day. The recommended calcium intake during pregnancy is approximately 1200 mg per day. Each serving from the milk group contains 300 mg. Dairy products are ideal because they contain not only calcium but vitamin D and lactose (or milk sugar), both of which also help the body absorb calcium.

Mothers who do not consume dairy products because of lactose intolerance need to look at alternative ways of getting calcium into their diets and should discuss this with a dietitian for a strategic plan. Enzyme supplements may help digest lactose. You can also buy dairy products which have had the lactose removed. Several good products are available in supermarkets, including chocolate milk. In these products, the lactose sugar has been split into two by an enzyme during processing, which may make them taste sweeter than the regular products. Naturally processed yogurt and most ripened cheeses contain little or no lactose and provide a good amount of calcium for mothers-to-be. That is because the little microbes that ripen cheese and form yogurt use up lactose as they ferment these products. Ripened cheeses include Cheddar, Swiss, Edam, Gouda, Muenster and Brick. Cottage cheese and cream cheese are not ripened and might cause some discomfort to lactose-intolerant women (In fact, cream cheese doesn't really belong in the same category with cheese at all. Since it is almost 50 percent fat, it should be considered in the same category as butter or margarine.) These two products are also rather low in calcium. In the case of cottage cheese, that is because the curds are separated from the whey, which contains calcium. Milk or cream added to the curds provides some additional calcium along with some lactose. However, dry cottage cheese has only a small amount of calcium to offer.

Some women may experience an improvement in their tolerance of lactose during pregnancy that allows them to consume more dairy foods without any discomfort.

Green leafy vegetables such as spinach, bok choy, and broccoli also provide calcium. So do salmon, sardines, and herring and other canned fishes (with bones left in). Sesame seeds are another popular source.

Calcium supplements may help those with special needs to get enough calcium. Teenagers, mothers who are expecting twins or triplets, and previous dieters who may have a history of low-calcium diets may all be candidates for calcium supplements. Add to this list women with frequent pregnancies, as well as those with lactose intolerance. However, all would be wise to try to increase their intake of dairy products in order to ensure adequate intakes of vitamin D as well as calcium.

Women who are pregnant or lactating need four servings of high-calcium foods each day. Each serving should contain 300 mg of calcium. The recipes in this section give you a fun and delicious way to get it all. Calcium-rich recipes at the end of this section contain tofu, broccoli, cheeses, sesame seeds, spinach, and milk.

Good Sources of Calcium	Amount Yielding Daily Requirement of Adult Female
Turnip greens, cooked	4 cups
Spinach, cooked	3¼ cups
Beet greens, cooked	5 cups
Broccoli, cooked	4½ cups
Parmesan cheese	¾ cup
Shrimp, boiled	9 ounces
1% low-fat milk	2½ cups
Buttermilk	2¾ cups
Romano cheese	2½ ounces
Swiss cheese	3 ounces
Muenster cheese	4 ounces
Sardines, canned with bones	8 ounces

Iron

Iron is extremely important for all of the changes taking place during pregnancy. It is an essential part of hemoglobin, which carries oxygen to each cell for energy metabolism. The increases in new tissue demand lots of iron. These include the developing infant, the increased blood supply to the placenta, and the increases in the mother's own body tissues.

Iron is perhaps the most common nutritional deficiency during pregnancy for North American women. Most women get barely enough iron before conception to sustain good body stores throughout their pregnancy. Many are on the verge of anemia. It's worth a routine blood test to find out if iron deficiency is causing problems of tiredness or fatigue. The need for iron during pregnancy is twice the usual requirement, so it's tough to get the necessary amounts without close attention to diet.

If you enter pregnancy with less than optimal iron stores in your body, you run the risk of developing anemia as soon as demands are made on those meagre stores. This is not just a problem that might occur during pregnancy. You can lose iron during surgery or other events which cause blood loss, such as accidents, extremely heavy menstrual flow, or bleeding ulcers. Therefore most women in North America can develop iron deficiency anemia at almost any time. All women should be evaluated for their iron status as a routine part of any regular medical exam, and especially during the early part of pregnancy.

The recommended intake for iron is hard to meet through a good diet alone. For this reason the United States National Academy of Sciences recommends that all pregnant women take 30 mg of iron a day in the form of a supplement from the twelfth week of pregnancy onward. This supplement should ideally be consumed between meals with foods that enhance its absorption. This includes orange juice or other foods high in vitamin C. Iron supplements should not be consumed with milk, tea, or coffee, which are known to reduce the iron's absorption. In addition to the supplement it is a good idea for women to follow a diet that is high in iron. This includes meats and seafood such as clams and oysters, which not only provide their own source of iron but also enhance the absorption of iron from other sources. We have some great recipes for clams and mussels at the end of this section. One of the best-known foods for boosting iron intake is liver, but European health authorities advise pregnant women against the use of animal liver because sections of it may have toxic levels of vitamin A. Eating pâté is not discouraged, because it is mixed with other ingredients and does not contain pockets of very high amounts of vitamin A. Other iron-rich foods are peas, beans, nuts, dried fruits, and breakfast cereals.

You should be checked for anemia more than once during pregnancy to ensure that you are getting adequate amounts of iron from your diet and from supplements. If you test positive for anemia, you may have to increase your daily intake of iron to 50 to 120 mg. This could mean swallowing several pills every day. Taking one pill every few hours rather than all the pills at once will help you reduce the nausea, heartburn, diarrhea, and other discomforts associated with the use of an iron supplement. Because they may be better tolerated at bed time, take at least one of the supplements at that time.

Without iron supplements a woman may take up to two years to get her body stores back to normal. A good iron intake during pregnancy will also help to provide good iron stores for the baby.

The baby's stores last for about four to six months after birth, when the infant begins to make his own supply of hemoglobin. Taking supplements will help to protect your baby as well as yourself from anemia.

Whenever we recommend a nutrient supplement, there is always room for some sort of caution. Just because "some is good" doesn't mean that "more is better." Never exceed the prescribed dosage. The use of a very high-iron supplement as prescribed for women with anemia may also lead to a reduction in the absorption of zinc. If you take a supplement, eat the recommended levels of meat, poultry, and seafood to get an adequate level of zinc into your diet.

Good Sources of Iron	Amount for Full Day's Requirement
Spinach, cooked	2½ cups
Oysters, raw	¾ cup
Sauerkraut, canned	4 cups
Green peas, cooked	5 cups
Braunschweiger sausage	5½ cups
Kidney beans, cooked	2½ cups
Lima beans, cooked	2½ cups
Navy beans, cooked	3 cups
Steak, beef	16 ounces
Prune juice	5 cups
Pot roast	13 ounces

Folate

Folate, also known as folic acid, is critical for the growth of all cells, especially the red blood cells, and for the development of new tissue. Some of the anemia which appears during pregnancy may be due to folate deficiency. However, folate supplements have been a concern in the past because their use may cover up a vitamin B_{12} deficiency known as pernicious anemia.

Within the last few years, a low intake of folic acid has been associated with neural tube defects (known as NTDs) in babies. The best known of these NTDs is spina bifida. Recent studies have shown that women who give birth to one child with an NTD have a better chance of giving birth to a child without one when they take folate supplements before and during pregnancy. As a result of these studies, the Food and Drug Administration in the United States and the British National Health Service have recommended that all women at risk of pregnancy should take a supplement of 0.4 mg folate each day and that women with a history of NTDs take ten times that amount (4 mg). Canadian experts have determined that supplementation should be strictly reserved for women who have had a previous pregnancy resulting in an NTD. They advise women to discuss the question with their physicians.

A debate is now under way on whether certain foods should be fortified with folate to prevent NTDs, just as milk is fortified with vitamin D to prevent rickets. A high folate intake is required at or before conception, however many women are not aware that they are pregnant until some time after conception.

The recommendation for folate during pregnancy is twice the usual intake. Therefore it is worth knowing how to eat enough to ensure an adequate intake from foods. Good sources of folate include orange juice, vegetables such as dark green lettuce, asparagus, and broccoli, as well as peanuts and cereals. With a daily intake of two servings of these sources, as suggested in the following table, women can get an adequate amount of folate during pregnancy.

The recipe section of this chapter has some excellent recipes for foods that are high in folate, including Cantaloupe Peach Soup; Spinach, Romaine, and Strawberry Salad; Thai Spinach Salad; and Spinach and Tofu in Phyllo.

Good Sources of Folate	Amount to Yield ½ of Daily Requirement
Spinach, fresh chopped	1¾ cups
Romaine lettuce, chopped	2½ cups
Spinach, cooked	¾ cup
Turnip greens, cooked	1 cup
Asparagus, cooked	1 cup
Broccoli, cooked	1¾ cups
Beets, cooked	2 cups
Orange juice	1¾ cups
Wheat germ, raw	¾ cup
Cantaloupe melon	1¼ melons
Beans, pinto	1½ cups
Sunflower seeds, oil-roasted	½ cup

Vitamin B_6

Your need for vitamin B_6 increases during pregnancy because of hormonal changes. Nausea and depression have been associated with changes in vitamin B_6 metabolism brought on by PMS, pregnancy, or the use of oral contraceptives. Although B_6 deficiencies are rare, your doctor may prescribe a vitamin B_6 supplement to correct these symptoms. The prescription might be in the range of 5 to 10 mg a day, which far exceeds the normal requirement for vitamin B_6, but is well below the toxic dosage.

Some time ago patients taking their own prescriptions of 1 to 2 grams of B_6 (several hundred times the 5 to 10 mg prescription) were afflicted with permanent nerve and liver damage. Remember never to exceed the recommended dosage. In order to increase your intake of vitamin B_6, eat more vegetables, meats, and fruits.

Vitamin B_{12}

Vitamin B_{12} is a special concern for women who have been strict vegetarians for more than a year. This vitamin is found mainly in foods of animal origin, such as milk, eggs, cheese, and meat. However, it may also be found in fermented vegetable-based foods such as miso, a fermented soya product. If you have not consumed these products for several years before pregnancy, you may require either a supplement or vitamin B_{12} injections. Even if you have no symptoms of a deficiency of vitamin B_{12} (anemia, weakness, or neurological problems), your baby may be born with inadequate stores to thrive during the first few months of breastfeeding. In one case in Los Angeles, a young infant who developed nerve damage in the first five months of life turned out to be suffering from a B_{12} deficiency. The deficiency was related to the vegan diet of the mother during pregnancy and breastfeeding. If you are a strict vegetarian, consult your doctor about B_{12} supplements.

Protein

Most women don't need to be especially concerned about getting adequate protein in their diets. In fact, most of us regularly eat twice the amount of protein we need.

In the early 1980s, researchers in New York City discovered that women taking protein supplements, in an effort to improve their babies' birth weights, actually had babies with lower weights. The reasons are not entirely clear, although it is fair to say that protein supplements are not recommended during pregnancy. However, if you are a very strict vegetarian, you should pay special attention to your protein intake. This could include careful blending of protein sources such as rice and beans or legumes and cereals to ensure that vegetable and grain sources offer the highest-quality protein. Combining complementing proteins will help you extend the protein value from vegetables and grains. Try the Easy Vegetarian Chili on p. 97 or Microwave Mushroom and Green Pea Risotto on p. 93.

Zinc

Zinc plays a very important role in fetal development. Studies in Scandinavia suggested that a low zinc intake may be associated with an increase in the number of birth defects. This makes zinc a nutrient worthy of attention. If you are pregnant, you should be consuming meat and dairy products in order to get the best available source of zinc.

There is no evidence to support the use of zinc supplements. In fact, mineral supplements can create problems, since several minerals use a similar route for absorption into the body. When too much of one mineral is available, it prevents others from being absorbed. For example, iron supplements can reduce zinc absorption and high zinc intake can compete with copper and iron. This is why you should never prescribe your own nutrient supplements. What appears to be a good thing may turn out to be harmful when used in excess.

Iodine

Iodine is an essential mineral for brain development, fetal development, and fetal survival, and was one of the first nutrients to be recognized for its role in causing birth defects when deficient. Although this is not a problem in North America, areas in the world where iodine is naturally deficient in the diet have very high numbers of babies born with cretinism. This syndrome includes mental retardation, abnormal thyroid function, and facial deformities. Since iodine supplementation has been introduced into these areas the number of infants born with cretinism has dropped. In North America, however, our diet is well supplied with iodine because we use iodized salt and eat foods with iodine-based preservatives in them.

Supplements

You will need multivitamin supplements if you're experiencing nausea and vomiting which keeps you from choosing a variety of balanced nutritious meals; if you have a history of weight reduction;

if you are under twenty; or if you are expecting twins (or more!).

Supplements and other drugs which are not specifically prescribed for pregnancy can bring with them a set of potential complications. For example, the derivative of vitamin A called isotretinoin, which is used to treat cystic acne, has caused serious birth defects or spontaneous abortions when taken by pregnant women. Very clear warnings are printed on the labels of these products of vitamin A–like compounds about the dangers to pregnant women. Other fat-soluble vitamins may cause damage to the developing fetus; however, there are no cases reported.

If you take large doses of water-soluble vitamins, the fetus may become conditioned to high doses of the vitamin before birth. For example, taking megadoses of vitamin C throughout pregnancy may mean that your baby will need higher than normal amounts of vitamin C. The higher level of vitamin C that the infant was used to in pregnancy cannot be provided through breastfeeding. As a result, your child might be at risk of scurvy, a deficiency of vitamin C. Only take a supplement if your doctor considers it necessary.

Other Concerns During Pregnancy

Salt

You don't need to restrict your salt consumption during pregnancy unless your doctor advises you to. Water retention is part of the normal prenatal experience and a minimum intake of sodium between 1 and 2 grams is advisable. Since most people consume up to 10 to

12 grams of sodium a day, you will probably get more than adequate amounts of sodium in your diet throughout pregnancy.

Caffeine

Animal studies show that extremely high levels of caffeine can cause problems with pregnancy. However, studies on humans have demonstrated that caffeine is not something for pregnant women to be especially concerned about. Still, many people wonder how much caffeine is too much. Experts say that an intake equivalent to two to four cups of coffee per day is reasonable. This includes all of the caffeine that would be found in coffee, colas, tea, and chocolate, or in medications such as cough medicines. Restricting caffeine during pregnancy may be a useful exercise in preparation for breastfeeding, since caffeine gets into breast milk and may keep your baby awake.

Heartburn

Heartburn is a problem that can develop at any point in pregnancy, but it may become noticeable after the nausea and vomiting subside. Typically it appears at about six months when the fetus is pressing against the diaphragm causing pressure on the stomach. Certain things, such as chocolate, will worsen the heartburn. Chocolate is a natural laxative which relaxes the upper passage into the stomach and allows the acidic contents to rise up and irritate the lower end of the esophagus.

If you use antacids to control heartburn, choose carefully. Calcium-based antacids can add to the total calcium intake and help to reduce the impact of heartburn at the same time. Although aluminum-based products may be effective in treating the symptoms, they may reduce the absorption of other nutrients.

Constipation

Constipation is a common problem during pregnancy and is caused by the changing levels of hormones. These hormones slow down the work of the digestive tract. The best way to deal with this is to increase the intake of fibre by eating lots of fruits and vegetables, high-fibre cereals, beans, and whole grains. Within each of these categories, there are certain foods that are particularly high in the type of fibre that will relieve constipation. Some examples are provided in the following table. Experts recommend 25–35 grams of fibre each day. Drink plenty of fluids and avoid laxatives if possible. They may create a problem of dependence, whereby the body loses its normal ability to pass waste. The most natural solutions are usually the best ones. We have included many delicious high-fibre recipes at the end of this chapter, such as White Bean Dip, Vegetable Soup, and Bran Muffins.

DIETARY FIBRE VALUES FOR FIBRE-CONTAINING FOODS

Food Group	Serving	Grams of Dietary Fibre
Breads and Cereals		
Air-popped popcorn	1 cup	2.5
All Bran	$\frac{1}{3}$ cup	8.5
Grapenuts	$\frac{1}{4}$ cup	1.4
Oatmeal (cooked)	1 cup	2.2
Whole-wheat bread	1 slice	1.4
Vegetables, cooked		
Broccoli	$\frac{1}{2}$ cup	2.2
Carrots	$\frac{1}{2}$ cup	2.3
Green peas	$\frac{1}{2}$ cup	3.6
Parsnip	$\frac{1}{2}$ cup	2.7
Potato, with skin	1 medium	2.5
Fruits		
Apple	1 medium	3.5
Banana	1 medium	2.4
Blueberries	$\frac{1}{2}$ cup	2.0
Orange	1 medium	2.6
Strawberries	1 cup	3.0

Cravings and aversions

You may experience unusual cravings during different times of your pregnancy. There does not appear to be any nutritional explanation for these cravings. If you crave specific foods, indulge yourself, but try to eat other foods to balance your cravings. For example, if you crave meat and cheese sandwiches, be sure to get a salad and fruit for dessert. If you crave sweets or salty chips, go ahead and have some, but eat them slowly and don't overdo it. A few women crave non-foods like laundry starch or clay. These are potentially harmful for the digestion of other nutrients and should be avoided.

Food aversions may also create some concern. The odour or sight of foods such as raw meats may make you feel nauseated. If so, bring home prepared foods or opt for alternatives such as eggs, tuna, or cheese until the stage passes.

Stress

The impact of stress on pregnancy has not been extensively examined. However, women under stress tend to have smaller babies and to deliver prematurely. Avoiding stress is easier to say than to do, but try to pace yourself, set reasonable goals, and learn to say no if your workload starts to get overwhelming. Try to maintain a healthy and normal routine and to present yourself in the most positive way. Some women really do blossom during pregnancy, others do not! Be fair to yourself and remember...this too shall pass.

Exercise

Many women are interested in continuing their exercise routines throughout pregnancy to enjoy the benefits of a healthy lifestyle. The effect of exercise on pregnancy has not been fully researched. However, there have been a number of elite athletes who continued training throughout most of pregnancy with good results. You need to know how your body is changing during pregnancy. For example, pregnancy will increase joint mobility and relaxation of the ligaments, which may increase your risk of sports injuries. You should also be aware of the risks of falls or other sports injuries when you are active.

Excessive exercise is a concern when it causes an increase in the core temperature of the body, since this could harm the developing fetus. For this reason, avoid saunas and steam baths which increase your internal temperature. Even moderate exercise over a long period of time may decrease the amount of oxygen flowing through the uterus to the fetus. In general, use common sense in any fitness program and exercise within a level of comfort to ensure that you do no harm to yourself or to your baby.

Some good examples of exercises to carry on throughout pregnancy are swimming and walking. The key to maintaining a healthy level of activity is to feel comfortable throughout the exercise. Be sure to discuss any concerns you may have with your doctor.

BEFORE THE BEGINNING

RECIPES

THESE RECIPES WERE GATHERED FROM MANY CORNERS OF THE world and designed with the needs of the expectant mother in mind. The emphasis is on great-tasting food that is easy to prepare and is loaded with good nutrition. Each recipe is a practical and delicious application of the nutrition information we have presented. Nutrition highlights are provided for many of the recipes.

You might find yourself with an appetite for the most exotic or the most simple of foods. You may be more comfortable spreading your meals out to include mid-morning and mid-afternoon snacks. You might find special comfort in the high-fibre foods designed with you in mind. The ideal foods to meet all of your special needs are in this section. But don't think of them in the same category as those maternity clothes you'll never wear again. These recipes are for now and always and will be a big hit with everyone in the family.

Using *Canada's Food Guide to Healthy Eating*, we recommend the following for pregnant or breastfeeding women:

Grain Products	9 to 12 servings a day
Vegetables and Fruits	8 to 10 servings a day
Milk Products	3 to 4 servings a day
Meat and Alternatives	2 to 3 servings a day

Grain Products

Canada's Food Guide to Healthy Eating recommends 5 to 12 servings of grain products each day. A serving is defined as one slice of bread, ⅔ cup (150 mL) cereal or ½ cup (125 mL) pasta or rice. For pregnant or breastfeeding women, the upper end of this range is a reasonable goal, as long as you keep in touch with your appetite.

At some time in recent history, the grain products acquired an unfounded reputation for being unhealthy and fattening. That was never true! Grain products are excellent sources of starch (important for energy) and fibre. Enriched and whole-grain products are especially good sources of iron and the B-vitamins (niacin, thiamin, and riboflavin).

Because grains are high in starch and generally low in fat, dietitians recommend eating more grains now than we have been eating. Eating more grains naturally causes us to eat less of the higher-fat foods. This should help us to change our meals to conform to the recommended shift to a lower-fat diet.

Plan meals around large servings of breads, cereals, rice, pasta, or corn-based products. Add plenty of vegetables and fruits and a 2 to 3 oz (50 to 75 g) serving from the meat and alternate group. Planning meals to take on these new proportions should help us to move creatively towards a healthier diet.

Look for other great grain recipes in Part 3.

Vegetables and Fruit

Canada's Food Guide to Healthy Eating recommends 5 to 10 servings a day from the vegetables and fruit group. A serving is defined as one fruit or a ½ cup (125 mL) serving of vegetables. Like the grain products, these are good sources of carbohydrates, everyone's favourite source of energy. The guide also recommends that we eat dark green and orange vegetables as often as possible. This is because of their high content of folate, beta-carotene, and minerals. Citrus fruits are also recommended because of the vitamin C content.

The benefits of fruits and vegetables cannot be overstated. New benefits are being discovered all the time. Foods of the onion family (garlic, onions, shallots) and the cabbage family (broccoli, cabbage, cauliflower, brussels sprouts) have received special attention. At this point, we are not recommending that you supplement your diet with the extracts of these foods, but that you make them an important part of your meal planning.

Vegetables and fruits can almost always be enjoyed in their raw form and should be eaten this way whenever possible. The recipes in this section were designed to give you some exciting options to make vegetables and fruits a great part of your menu.

Milk Products

Milk products are the major source of calcium in the Canadian diet. In addition, they supply an important source of riboflavin, protein, and vitamin D. *Canada's Food Guide to Healthy Eating* recommends 2 to 4 servings a day and suggests that we choose lower-fat products more often. Pregnant and breast-feeding women need 3 to 4 servings a day. A serving size is defined as one cup (250 mL) milk, ¾ cup (175 mL) yogurt, or two slices of cheese.

Milk products include cheese, yogurt, and ice cream. Several of these foods have been combined in recipes with those of the other food groups. See the fruit soups with yogurt for additional examples. Many of the hot vegetable main courses include cheese and/or pasta or rice, giving you a two-in-one or three-in-one bonus.

If dairy fat is a concern, any of the recipes can be made with lower-fat cheeses, yogurt, or milk. There are more tasty varieties on the market every month.

Meats and Alternatives

The meat and alternatives group includes a wide variety of choices. Everything from meat, poultry, and fish to eggs and legumes belongs to this food group. Legumes are a group of high-protein, high-fibre seeds of plants. Some examples include peanuts, soybeans, lima beans, peas, and other beans. The products of these legumes, such as peanut butter and tofu, are also included. Tofu is derived from soybeans.

The recommended intake during pregnancy and breastfeeding is 3 servings a day. The serving size is defined as 2 to 4 oz (50 to 100 g) of meat, fish, or poultry and ½ to 1 cup (125 to 250 mL) of beans. Consider the average restaurant serving size for some of these foods. The typical steak size of 10 to 16 oz (250 to 400 g) may represent as many as four servings at one sitting!

This food group is a valuable source of many key nutrients. They include protein, fat, B-vitamins (especially folate and B_{12}), and minerals (especially iron, zinc, and magnesium). The legumes also add an excellent source of fibre. We have provided recipes for a wide range of foods from the meats and alternatives which can be used as appetizers, soups, and salads, as well as main courses.

The following meal plan provides an example of a typical day using recipes from this book and the recommended number of servings found within each food group.

Breakfast

orange juice
2⁄3 cup (150 mL) Granola (*p.57*)
Carrot and Banana Bread *(p. 56)* with peanut butter
1 cup (250 mL) milk

Snack

Apricot Bread *(p. 53)*
1 cup (250 mL) milk

Lunch

Carrot Ginger Soup *(p. 72)*
Easy Vegetarian Chili *(p. 97)*
Cornbread *(p. 209)* (2 slices)
Peach Slices with Yogurt

Snack

Chèvre with Pesto *(p. 59)* on rice crackers

Dinner

New Wave Caesar Salad *(p. 81)*
Tomato Bruschetta with Roasted Garlic *(p. 58)*
Pasta with Sun-dried Tomatoes and Vegetables *(p. 103)*
Swordfish with Apricot Sauce *(p. 112)*
Triple Berry Crisp *(p. 124)*

Snack

fresh fruit salad

Apricot Bread

Fruit breads are a good source of starch and improve in flavour as they age...but don't be surprised if this one doesn't last very long.

½ lb (250 g) dried apricots	Chop by hand or in a food processor.
½ cup (125 mL) orange juice	Heat in large bowl in microwave, about 10 seconds on Medium.
¾ cup (175 mL) brown sugar	Add to orange juice. Add apricots and set aside.
2 eggs, beaten until frothy 3 tbsp (50 mL) oil ½ cup (125 mL) buttermilk	Combine.
2 cups (500 mL) flour ¾ cup (175 mL) oatmeal, ground fine 2½ tsp (12 mL) baking powder ½ tsp (2 mL) baking soda ½ tsp (2 mL) salt	Mix together. Combine with egg mixture. Add egg mixture to apricot mixture.
½ cup (125 mL) chopped toasted almonds	Fold into batter.
	Pour into 9 x 5-inch (2 L) loaf pan and bake at 350°F (180°C) for 50 minutes to 1 hour, or until a toothpick inserted into the mixture comes out clean. MAKES ONE LARGE LOAF—10–12 SERVINGS.

Banana Pecan Bread

This is a great way to use up those overripe bananas and is a good source of starch and potassium.

¾ cup (175 mL) sugar 4 tbsp (60 mL) soft butter or margarine	Cream well.
3 medium bananas, mashed	Add to butter and sugar
1 egg, beaten 2 cups (500 mL) flour ⅓ cup (75 mL) buttermilk 1½ tsp (7 mL) baking powder ½ tsp (2 mL) baking soda ½ tsp (2 mL) salt	Mix together, then add to banana mixture.
1 cup (250 mL) chopped pecans	Add.
	Pour into 9 x 5-inch (2 L) loaf pan and bake at 350°F (180°C) for 1 hour, or until tester inserted in centre comes out clean. MAKES 10 SLICES.

Raspberry-Blueberry Cornmeal Muffins

Keep a muffin or two with you at work or when you are out and about. When you start to feel a little light-headed, nauseated, or hungry, this will help you make it to the next meal.

1 cup (250 mL) cornmeal 1 cup (250 mL) flour 1/3 cup (75 mL) sugar 2 tsp (10 mL) baking powder 1/4 tsp (1 mL) salt	Sift dry ingredients together in bowl.
1 cup (250 mL) buttermilk 6 tbsp (100 mL) melted butter 1 egg, lightly beaten	Form a well in dry ingredients and add combined liquids, stirring until just blended.
1 cup (250 mL) fresh or frozen blueberries 1/2 cup (125 mL) fresh or frozen raspberries	Fold in gently until just combined.
	Butter muffin tin, or use paper liners. Fill muffin tins 2/3 full. Bake 20 to 25 minutes at 400°F (200°C), or until tops of muffins spring back when lightly touched. MAKES 1 DOZEN LARGE MUFFINS.

Carrot and Banana Bread

This recipe is a high-nutrition way to get rid of those overripe bananas. If you have several of them, make two loaves and freeze one.

¾ cup (175 mL) sugar 4 tbsp (60 mL) unsalted butter	Cream until fluffy.
2 large eggs	Add, one at a time, and beat.
1 cup (250 mL) mashed bananas (about 2 medium)	Add.
2 cups (500 mL) flour 2 tsp (10 mL) baking powder ¾ tsp (4 mL) cinnamon ½ tsp (2 mL) salt ¼ tsp (1 mL) nutmeg Pinch ground cloves	Sift together and add to banana mixture.
¾ cup (175 mL) chopped walnuts ¾ cup (175 mL) grated carrots 1 tsp (5 mL) vanilla	Add and mix well.
	Pour into 9 x 5-inch (2 L) loaf pan and bake at 350°F (180°C) for 1 hour, or until tester inserted in centre comes out clean. Let rest 15 minutes, then cool on rack before serving. MAKES 10 SLICES.

Granola

Oats are a great source of soluble fibre. The nuts, seeds, and powdered milk make this a good source of protein. With a bowl of this for breakfast, you will feel sustained all morning long.

5 cups (1.25 L) rolled oats 1 cup (250 mL) chopped almonds 1 cup (250 mL) sunflower seeds 1 cup (250 mL) wheat germ 1 cup (250 mL) instant powdered milk	Mix together.
¾ cup (175 mL) honey ½ cup (125 mL) vegetable oil	Heat together on medium heat until honey is runny and add to above.
½ cup (125 mL) dried apricots ½ cup (125 mL) raisins ½ cup (125 mL) chopped dates	Combine with honey-oat mixture.
	Spread onto 2 to 3 cookie sheets. Bake at 325°F (160°C) for 45 minutes, or until browned. MAKES 10 CUPS OR 20 ½ CUP SERVINGS.

Tomato Bruschetta with Roasted Garlic

A very flavourful hors d'oeuvre and also great as a lunch with a green salad.

2 lbs (1 kg) tomatoes, peeled, seeded, and diced (about 6 medium)	Place in non-aluminum colander. Let drain 10 minutes. Put into large bowl.
¼ cup (50 mL) chopped basil 1 tsp (5 mL) salt 3 tbsp (50 mL) olive oil	Add to tomatoes and set aside.
6 cloves garlic, unpeeled 1 tbsp (15 mL) olive oil	Toss garlic and oil together, then place garlic on baking sheet. Roast at 375°F (190°C) for 10 to 12 minutes, or until soft. Cool slightly, then peel and chop coarsely. Toss tomatoes with roasted garlic.
1 baguette, sliced diagonally into 15 slices	Toast bread slices 30 seconds on each side under broiler. Remove from oven. Spoon 1 to 2 tbsp (15 to 25 mL) tomato mixture onto each slice.
15 tsp (75 mL) grated Parmesan cheese	Sprinkle 1 tsp (15 mL) Parmesan cheese on each slice. Return to oven for about 3 minutes, or until cheese begins to melt.
	MAKES 15 PIECES.

Chèvre with Pesto

Denise Brzezinski gave us this recipe several years ago. Watch out! It's addictive.

6 oz (300 g) chèvre, formed into a ball 1 tbsp (15 mL) olive oil	Roll cheese in oil.
¼ cup (50 mL) chopped pecans ¼ cup (50 mL) mustard seeds 1 tbsp (15 mL) coarsely ground black pepper	Mix pecans, seeds, and pepper together. Roll cheese in pecan mixture.
10 oz (284 mL) package frozen spinach ½ cup (125 mL) pesto sauce 1 tbsp (15 mL) rice vinegar	Blend spinach, pesto, and vinegar in a food processor.
⅓ cup (75 mL) olive oil	Slowly add olive oil to spinach mixture.
	Place spinach mixture on 8-inch (20 cm) serving platter. Spread to edges. Heat cheese at 400°F (200°C) for 4 to 5 minutes. Carefully place cheese on spinach mixture. The spinach mixture can be warmed in a microwave for 20 seconds on Medium. SERVES 2 OR 4 DEPENDING ON APPETITE.

Goat Cheese (Chèvre) Spread

This is a light and simple hors d'oeuvre spread. As a variation, spread it on a slice of baguette and warm it in a 350°F (180°C) oven for 2 to 3 minutes.

⅓ cup (75 mL) sun-dried tomatoes ⅓ cup (75 mL) boiling water	Soak tomatoes in water. Let sit 5 minutes, drain, and pat dry.
8 oz (200 g) goat cheese 4 cloves garlic, minced	Mix in food processor with tomatoes.
	Serve in a bowl, with whole wheat baguette rounds or toast. MAKES HORS D'OEUVRES TO SERVE 4.

Imitation Liver

This is an unbelievably delicious hors d'oeuvre spread which has the taste and texture of Jewish chopped liver.

1 14-oz (398 ml) can green beans	Strain beans and press out moisture.
1 large onion, chopped 1 tbsp (15 mL) olive oil	Sauté onion in oil.
3 hard-cooked eggs ½ cup (125 mL) walnuts 1 to 2 tbsp (15 to 25 mL) mayonnaise Salt and pepper to taste	Grind beans, onion, eggs, and walnuts in a blender or food processor with enough mayonnaise to make a firm mixture.
	Decorate with parsley and cherry tomatoes. SERVES 4 TO 6 AS AN HORS D'OEUVRE.

White Bean Dip

White beans are high in fibre and protein and low in fat.

15 oz (435 g) can white kidney beans 4 tsp (20 mL) lemon juice 3 cloves garlic, minced	Blend in food processor.
2 tbsp (25 mL) olive oil 1 tsp (5 mL) ground cumin ½ tsp (2 mL) chili powder 1 tbsp parsley, minced Salt and pepper to taste	Add and process until blended.
1 tbsp (15 mL) minced cilantro	Add.
	Serve with fresh carrot sticks, broccoli, green beans, celery, cauliflower, or tortilla chips. Serves 4 to 6 as an hors d'oeuvre.

Mushroom Nut Pâté

The nuts and yogurt make this a high-protein, high-nutrient snack.

1 large onion, finely chopped 2 cloves garlic, minced 1 tbsp vegetable oil	Sauté onion and garlic in oil for 5 minutes.
1 lb (500 g) mushrooms, chopped 2 tbsp (25 mL) lemon juice 1 tsp (5 mL) basil, dried ½ tsp (2 mL) thyme	Add to onions and garlic. Heat until liquid is completely reduced. Set aside to cool.
½ lb (500 g) walnuts ¼ lb (250 g) hazelnuts ¾ lb (250 g) almonds	Toast nuts for 8 minutes at 350° F, then reduce to powder in a food processor. Set aside.
1 large bunch parsley 1½ cups (375 mL) yogurt 1½ tsp (7 mL) lemon juice ¼ tsp (1 mL) salt ¼ tsp (1 mL) pepper	Mix together in a large stainless steel bowl. Blend in food processor until smooth. Add onion and nut mixtures and process. Chill.
	Serve on whole wheat bread or crackers. SERVES 6 TO 8 AS AN HORS D'OEUVRE.

Clams Steamed in Champagne

Clams are an excellent source of iron. One 3 oz (75 g) serving has 25 mg iron, which is almost as much as you'd get from an iron supplement. The iron in clams is also very easily absorbed. When champagne is heated, the alcohol disappears, leaving the flavour behind.

3 tbsp (50 mL) olive oil	Heat oil in heavy pot.
½ lb (250 g) well-scrubbed clams 4 cloves garlic, minced	Add clams and garlic and cook for 2 minutes.
¾ cup (175 mL) champagne or sparkling white wine 2 green onions, finely chopped	Add wine and onions, cover, and steam for 5 minutes. Remove any unopened clams and discard. Remove remaining clams and set aside in a covered dish. Cook remaining liquid on medium-high heat for 5 minutes, or until reduced to ½ cup (125 mL).
2 tbsp (25 mL) butter	Whisk in butter a little at a time.
2 tbsp (25 mL) chopped parsley 1 tsp (5 mL) lemon juice	Add to champagne mixture. Pour mixture over clams and serve.
	SERVES 2.

Steamed Clams
and Spicy Fennel

Chock full of iron and flavourful fennel, which has a subtle licorice flavour.

2 tbsp (25 mL) olive oil	Heat in saucepan.
3 cloves garlic, minced ¾ tsp (4 mL) dried oregano ½ tsp (2 mL) dried basil ¼ to ½ tsp (1 to 2 mL) dried hot pepper flakes	Add to oil and cook over medium heat.
1 cup (250 mL) thinly sliced fennel bulbs ½ cup (125 mL) chopped onion dry white wine 1 14-oz (398 ml) can plum tomatoes, chopped	Add to garlic and herbs and sauté until fennel is softened (about 4 to 5 minutes). Add to fennel mixture and cook for 5 minutes.
30 clams, scrubbed well	Add to fennel and tomato mixture, cover, and continue cooking for 5 to 7 minutes, or until clams have opened. Discard any unopened clams.
	Remove to serving platter and garnish with parsley. Serve with crusty bread or on a bed of pasta. SERVES 2.

Saffron Mussels

Mussels are a good source of iron and zinc and an excellent source of folate and vitamin B$_{12}$.

½ cup (125 mL) chopped onion 2 cloves garlic, minced 1 tbsp (15 mL) olive oil	Sauté onions and garlic in oil until soft.
1 cup (250 mL) chopped tomatoes ½ cup (125 mL) white wine ½ cup (125 mL) water ½ tsp (2 mL) saffron	Add to onions and let simmer for 5 minutes.
2 lbs (1 kg) mussels	Add to wine mixture and cover. Steam for 5 to 7 minutes, or until mussels open. Discard unopened mussels.
	Serve with crusty bread. SERVES 2.

My Basic Vegetable Stock

Simmer soups gently on the lowest heat that will sustain a bubble. This will cut down on vitamin losses because a vigorous boil exposes them to more air bubbles, which cause destruction by oxidation.

3 qts (3 L) water

4 large carrots, peeled and cut into chunks

3 stalks celery, coarsely chopped

1 apple, cut into chunks (unpeeled)

1 large onion, coarsely chopped

10 peppercorns

6 sprigs parsley

1 bay leaf

Wash all vegetables. Put vegetables and herbs in water and simmer for 45 minutes to 1 hour. Strain and use for making soup.

Feel free to throw in dried-up bits of carrots, celery, parsley stems, or onion.

MAKES 10 CUPS OF STOCK.

Pesto and Vegetable Soup

Carrots are a great source of beta-carotene and fibre. The garbanzo beans add protein and insoluble fibre and the broccoli adds calcium, beta-carotene, folate, and vitamin C.

1 cup (250 mL) chopped onions 3 tbsp (50 mL) olive oil	Sauté onions in oil until soft.
2 carrots, chopped 1 small red pepper, chopped	Add to onions and sauté for 3 to 4 minutes.
5 cups (1.25 L) vegetable stock 1½ cups (375 mL) broccoli florets 1 cup (250 mL) chopped zucchini 1 cup (250 mL) garbanzo beans 1 cooking potato, peeled and diced	Add to onions, carrots, and pepper and bring to a boil. Reduce heat and simmer for 15 minutes.
¼ to ⅓ cup (50 to 75 mL) pesto Salt and pepper to taste	Stir into vegetable mixture.
	SERVES 4 TO 6 DEPENDING ON APPETITE.

Black Bean Soup

Black beans are a good source of starch, protein, and fibre. To balance the strong flavour of this soup, serve it with fresh rolls.

1 lb (500 g) dried black beans	Rinse beans 3 times and remove any stones. Put into a large saucepan.
5 qts (5 L) water ½ cup (125 mL) tomato purée 1½ tsp (7 mL) salt 1 tsp (5 mL) cumin 1 tsp (5 mL) oregano 1 tsp (5 mL) coriander seeds ½ tsp (2 mL) thyme 3 cloves garlic, minced	Add to beans and bring to a boil. Lower heat and simmer for 3 hours or until beans have softened.
	Take 2 cups (500 mL) of the bean mixture and purée in a blender. Return to pot. For a completely smooth soup, purée the entire contents of the pot. SERVES 6 TO 8 DEPENDING ON APPETITE.

Minestrone Soup

A hearty soup. Feel free to throw in everything but the kitchen sink. This soup is a great opportunity to use up leftovers.

2 small onions, chopped 2 cloves garlic, minced 2 tbsp (25 mL) olive oil	In a large pot, sauté garlic and onions in oil for 3 to 4 minutes.
3 stalks celery, chopped 2 cups (500 mL) coarsely chopped zucchini 1 cup (250 mL) sliced mushrooms	Add to onions and garlic and cook for 2 to 3 minutes.
10 cups (2.5 L) vegetable broth 4 cups (1 L) peeled and chopped tomatoes 3 carrots, peeled and chopped 1 red pepper, chopped 1 tsp (5 mL) dried basil, or 1 tbsp fresh ½ tsp (2 mL) marjoram ½ tsp (2 mL) chili oil ¼ tsp (1 mL) thyme Bay leaf Salt and pepper to taste	Add, bring mixture to a boil, then reduce heat and simmer for 25 minutes.
1½ cups (375 mL) garbanzo beans 1½ cup (375 mL) small pasta shells, cooked	Add to vegetables and herbs, and cook for another 5 minutes, or until beans and pasta are hot. Ladle into bowls.
½ cup (125 mL) grated Parmesan cheese	Sprinkle 1 tbsp (15 mL) cheese on each bowl of soup.
	SERVES 8.

Simple Lentil Vegetable Soup

This soup makes a complete meal when you add bread and fruit salad for dessert.

2 to 3 tbsp (25 to 50 mL) olive oil	Heat oil in large saucepan.
1 large onion, chopped 1 red pepper, chopped 3 to 4 cloves garlic, minced	Add to oil and sauté until tender.
8 to 10 cups (2 to 2.5 L) water 1 ½ cups (375 mL) lentils 1 cup (250 mL) brown rice, uncooked 1 cup (250 mL) dry white wine 2 14-oz (398 ml) cans tomato sauce 3 large carrots, chopped 3 celery stalks, chopped 3 large red potatoes, diced 2 medium zucchinis, chopped 2 tsp (10 mL) dried basil 1 tsp (5 mL) dried thyme	Add to onion mixture. Cover saucepan. Simmer about 1¼ hours, or until lentils and rice are tender.
	SERVES 8.

Carrot Ginger Soup

This soup is loaded with vitamins and minerals. We made this on "The Journal" and got a great response. Eat the parsley too!

6 cups (1.5 L) water 6 large carrots, whole 3 stalks celery, whole 1 onion, whole	Cook vegetables in 2-quart (2 L) saucepan for 15 minutes, or until carrots are tender. Remove carrots from liquid and place in blender with 2 cups (500 mL) of strained liquid. Blend until puréed. Set aside remaining water and vegetables for other uses.
1 to 2 cups (500 mL to 1 L) buttermilk	Keep blender running and slowly add buttermilk.
1 tbsp (15 mL) grated gingerroot	Add ginger to blender. Return carrot-buttermilk mixture to saucepan and cook over medium heat until reheated.
	Serve with parsley sprigs. SERVES 4.

Broccoli Soup

This soup is an excellent source of calcium, beta-carotene, and folate, and a good source of iron.

2½ lbs broccoli	Wash and cut broccoli into chunks. Microwave on high for 5 minutes. Set aside.
2 tbsp margarine	Melt.
2 tbsp flour	Add to margarine and stir for at least 1 minute.
3 cups (750 mL) 2% milk	Gradually add milk, stirring constantly.
¼ tsp grated nutmeg Salt Pepper	Add. Pour all ingredients into blender and blend until puréed. Return to a saucepan.
1–2 cups vegetable stock	Add vegetable stock until desired consistency is reached.
	SERVES 4 TO 6.

August Soup

The cantaloupe and peaches are an excellent source of beta-carotene, folate, and iron. Yogurt adds protein, calcium, vitamin B$_{12}$, and zinc. The alcohol content of a serving is equal to the equivalent of one-sixth of an alcoholic beverage.

2 cups (500 mL) 2% yogurt

2 ripe peaches, peeled and pitted

1 ripe cantaloupe, cut into chunks

2 tbsp (25 mL) amaretto liqueur (optional)

1 tbsp (15 mL) lemon juice

1 tsp (5 mL) almond extract

¼ tsp (1 mL) cinnamon

Put ingredients in a food processor or blender and purée.

Chill 2 to 4 hours. Serve cold.

SERVES 6.

Papaya Yogurt Soup

Papayas are a good source of iron and niacin and an excellent source of vitamin C. Yogurt adds calcium, protein, and riboflavin.

1 lb (500 g) papaya, peeled, seeded, and cut into pieces

1 to 1 ½ cups (250 to 375 mL) 2% milk

1 cup (250 mL) plain yogurt

3 tbsp (50 mL) sugar

Pinch cinnamon

Pinch grated nutmeg

Purée in blender or processor until smooth. Chill.

Garnish with a slice of lime.

SERVES 4.

Cold Beet Borscht

Beets are a good source of beta-carotene and vitamin C and an excellent source of folate. The fat-free buttermilk adds calcium, protein, and riboflavin.

1 14-oz (398 mL) can sliced beets 1 tsp (5 mL) sugar	Purée in blender or food processor.
2 cups (500 mL) buttermilk	Keep food processor or blender running and slowly add buttermilk.
Salt and pepper to taste finely chopped cucumber 4 tbsp (60 mL) plain yogurt	Add. Cover and refrigerate until cold (about 2 hours). Ladle soup into bowls and garnish with cucumber and a dollop of yogurt.
	Serves 4.

Cantaloupe Peach Soup

Cantaloupe is a very good source of folate, beta-carotene, and vitamin C.

1 ripe cantaloupe, cut into chunks	Blend in food processor until purée forms.
2 ripe peaches, peeled and sliced ½ cup (125 mL) freshly squeezed orange juice 2 tbsp (25 mL) lime juice	Add to cantaloupe and purée.
	Chill 1 hour. Garnish with a dollop of yogurt in centre of bowl. SERVES 4.

Gazpacho

The small amount of wine in this recipe should not pose any problems, but if you want the flavour and none of the alcohol, boil the wine for a few minutes, then cool it and add to the recipe. Alcohol evaporates when heated.

3 cups (750 mL) tomatoes, peeled and seeded

1½ cups (375 mL) chopped English cucumbers

1 cup (250 mL) tomato juice

½ cup (125 mL) chopped onion

2 stalks celery, chopped

1 red pepper, chopped

3 tbsp (50 mL) olive oil

3 tbsp (50 mL) red wine vinegar

¼ cup (50 mL) dry white wine

2 tbsp (25 mL) parsley

2 cloves garlic, minced

Juice of ½ lemon

Salt and pepper to taste

Purée in food processor or blender.

Refrigerate for 6 to 8 hours. Garnish with croutons and Parmesan.

SERVES 8.

Spinach, Romaine, and Strawberry Salad with Poppyseed Dressing

This Winnipeg recipe is a popular salad in the winter when salads remind us of summer and in the strawberry season to take advantage of the delicious berries.

1 head romaine lettuce, washed and broken ½ bunch spinach, washed and broken 1 cup (250 mL) sliced strawberries ¼ cup (50 mL) thinly sliced purple onions	Toss together and set aside.
1 cup (250 mL) light mayonnaise ½ cup (125 mL) milk (2% or Homo) ¼ cup (50 mL) raspberry vinegar ⅓ cup (75 mL) sugar 2 tbsp (25 mL) poppyseeds	Mix together to make dressing. Toss with salad.
	MAKES 6 TO 8 SERVINGS.

Corn and Bell Pepper Salad

Corn is a good source of starch and fibre and is low in fat.

10 oz (250 g) corn, cooked and drained	Combine ingredients.
1 red pepper, diced	
1 green onion, chopped	
1/2 green pepper, diced	
2 tbsp (25 mL) cilantro, chopped	
2 tbsp (25 mL) olive oil	
1 tbsp (15 mL) lime juice	
1/4 tsp (1 mL) cumin	
Salt and pepper to taste	
Curly red lettuce leaves	Serve on curly red lettuce leaves.
	SERVES 2 TO 4—DEPENDING ON APPETITE.

New Wave Caesar Salad

We've combined spinach and romaine lettuce for more colour and texture than a traditional caesar. The balsamic vinegar adds lots of flavour.

1 tbsp (15 mL) butter 2 tbsp (25 mL) oil 1 tbsp (15 mL) fresh parsley, chopped 2 cloves garlic, minced	Melt butter in skillet, then add oil, parsley, and garlic and sauté.
8 slices French bread, cubed	Toss bread cubes in garlic mixture, coating thoroughly. Place on cookie sheet and bake at 350°F (180°C) for 10–15 minutes, or until crisp.
Dressing: ⅔ cup (150 mL) olive oil ¼ cup (50 mL) balsamic vinegar 1 egg, coddled in boiling water for 20 seconds 1 to 2 tsp (5 to 10 mL) anchovy paste 1 tsp (5 mL) Dijon mustard 1 clove garlic, minced ½ tsp (2 mL) salt ½ tsp (2 mL) pepper	Combine in blender and process well.
1 head romaine lettuce 1 bunch fresh spinach	Wash, dry, and tear greens into bite-sized pieces. Pour dressing over greens. Add croutons and toss.
½ cup (125 mL) grated Parmesan cheese	Sprinkle over salad.
	SERVES 8.

Thai Spinach Salad

Spinach is an excellent source of folate, calcium, and beta-carotene. This is our favourite new salad. Try adding crunchy Chinese noodles for an even more exciting texture.

1 large bunch of spinach	Remove stems and wash well. Cut into ribbons.
1 cup (250 mL) fresh bean sprouts ½ cup (125 mL) slivered white mushrooms ½ cup (125 mL) slivered toasted almonds 1 red pepper, sliced	Toss with spinach.
Dressing: 3 tbsp (50 mL) lime juice ¼ cup (50 mL) peanut oil 2 tbsp (25 mL) brown sugar 1 tbsp (15 mL) minced fresh mint leaves, or 1 tbsp (15 mL) mint sauce 1 tbsp (15 mL) minced fresh basil 1½ tsp (7 mL) minced gingerroot ½ tsp (2 mL) Chinese chili garlic sauce Pinch grated nutmeg	Mix together. Pour over the spinach salad.
	MAKES 4 TO 6 SERVINGS.

Spinach Salad with Cashews, Apples, and Mango Chutney Dressing

This salad has all of my favourite ingredients. Feel free to experiment with different nuts. Toasted peanuts work beautifully and so do toasted almonds.

1 bunch spinach	Remove stems and wash.
1 cup (250 mL) whole roasted cashews ¼ cup (50 mL) chopped green onion 1 tart green apple, coarsely chopped ½ sliced mango	Toss with spinach.
Dressing: 2 tbsp (25 mL) lemon juice 2 tbsp (25 mL) mango chutney 1 tbsp (15 mL) red wine vinegar ½ tsp (2 mL) curry powder ¼ tsp (1 mL) sugar ¼ tsp (1 mL) salt Pinch cayenne pepper Pinch turmeric	Combine in blender and process for 2 minutes.
⅓ cup (75 mL) light vegetable oil	Keep blender going, and gradually add oil until mixture is smooth.
	Toss salad with dressing and serve immediately. SERVES 4.

Vegetable and Wild Rice Salad

Perfect as a side dish for meat, poultry, fish, or add a scrambled egg for a complete meal.

2 cups (500 mL) vegetable or chicken broth 1 cup (250 mL) wild rice	Bring broth to a boil. Stir in rice. Reduce to medium heat and simmer 1 hour, or until rice is tender.
2 cups (500 mL) broccoli florets ½ lb (250 g) asparagus, cut into small pieces diagonally ½ cup (125 mL) green beans, cut diagonally 2 medium carrots, peeled and sliced	Cook vegetables in a separate pot of boiling water.
1 tomato, peeled, seeded, and chopped 4 oz (100 g) blue cheese, grated or crumbled	Combine with vegetables and rice and toss.
Dressing: 3 tbsp (50 mL) olive oil 2 tbsp (25 mL) lemon juice 1 tsp (5 mL) Dijon mustard Salt and pepper to taste	Mix together, and toss thoroughly with vegetables and rice.
	SERVES 4.

Indonesian Vermicelli Salad

This recipe has lots of crunch and lots of flavour.

1 lb (500 g) vermicelli	Cook vermicelli in boiling salted water for 10 minutes. Drain and set aside.
1 small head bok choy, coarsely chopped 1 small head sui choy, coarsely chopped 2 lbs (1 kg) broccoli, cut into bite-sized pieces 1 large bunch green onions, chopped 6 oz (150 g) bean sprouts 1 bunch radishes, finely sliced	Combine vegetables in large bowl. Set aside.
Dressing: ½ cup (125 mL) peanut oil ¼ cup (50 mL) red wine vinegar 2 tbsp (25 mL) fresh lemon juice 2 tbsp (25 mL) low-sodium soy sauce ½ tsp (2 mL) cayenne 1 clove garlic, minced Dash Worcestershire sauce Salt and pepper to taste	Blend in food processor or blender.
⅓ cup (75 mL) unsweetened peanut butter ⅓ cup (75 mL) water	Add to dressing and blend well. Toss vegetables and vermicelli with dressing.
½ cup (125 mL) toasted cashews	Sprinkle over salad.
	SERVES 8 TO 10.

French Green Beans with Balsamic Vinaigrette

This is my stepson Soleil's favourite salad dressing. He loves it on tomatoes, lettuce, and all vegetables.

1 lb (500 g) tiny French green beans	Boil beans in water for 6 to 7 minutes, or until tender. Set aside.
Balsamic vinaigrette: 2 tbsp (25 mL) balsamic vinegar 1 tsp (5 mL) Dijon mustard ¼ tsp (1 mL) salt 1 clove garlic, minced	Whisk together.
4 tbsp (60 mL) olive oil Freshly ground pepper Sugar to taste, about ¼ tsp (1 mL)	Continue whisking mustard mixture and gradually add the oil, drop by drop.
	Place beans on platter in neat row. Drizzle vinaigrette on top. SERVES 4 TO 6.

Couscous and Chickpea Salad

Easy to make! This dish has lots of fibre and protein and is always a winner in our home.

Ingredients	Instructions
1¾ cups (425 mL) water ½ tsp (2 mL) salt 6 oz (150 g) couscous	Bring salted water to boil. Add couscous. Cover. Remove from heat, and let sit for 5 minutes. Transfer to bowl and fluff with fork.
1 14-oz (398 mL) can garbanzo beans, drained and rinsed 1 cup (250 mL) finely chopped carrots 1 large red pepper, chopped 4 green onions, chopped 4 tbsp (60 mL) finely chopped parsley	Toss with couscous. Set aside.
Dressing: ½ cup (125 mL) mint leaves 3 tbsp (50 mL) lemon juice 1 tsp (5 mL) Dijon mustard ½ tsp (2 mL) sugar 1 clove garlic, minced	Blend in food processor or blender using on/off pulse.
½ cup (125 mL) olive oil	Gradually add oil to dressing while blending. Toss with couscous mixture. Serve on a bed of lettuce.
6 oz (150 g) feta cheese	Crumble on top of couscous.
	SERVES 4.

Curried Chicken Salad

This is another often-requested recipe from the Lazy Gourmet. (The Lazy Gourmet is a take out gourmet deli and catering company in Vancouver, B.C., owned by Susan Mendelson.)

2 cups (500 mL) diced cooked chicken

2 cups (500 mL) chopped celery

1 cup (250 mL) red bell pepper, seeded and chopped

1 cup (250 mL) green bell pepper, seeded and chopped

1 cup (250 mL) chopped mushrooms

1/2 cup (125 mL) coarsely chopped toasted almonds

1/2 cup (125 mL) red seedless grapes, halved

1/2 cup (125 mL) snow peas, lightly steamed

1/4 cup (50 mL) chopped fresh parsley

1/4 cup (50 mL) chopped red onion

Combine ingredients in a large bowl.

Dressing:

2/3 cup (150 mL) light mayonnaise

1/2 cup (125 mL) soft cream cheese

1/2 cup (125 mL) plain yogurt

2 tsp (10 mL) curry powder

1 tsp to 1 tbsp (5 to 15 mL) honey, to taste

2 dashes Tabasco sauce

Salt and freshly ground pepper to taste

Whisk together in separate bowl until well blended. Toss dressing with salad.

Serve dressed salad in melon halves.

SERVES 8.

Tuna Pasta Salad

A light and tasty lunch.

1 ½ cup cooked rotini

4 oz white tuna

2 tbsp diced red onion

2 tbsp diced red pepper

½ cup sliced French-style beans, cooked well

3 cherry tomatoes

1 tbsp capers

1 tbsp freshly squeezed lemon juice

2 tbsp olive oil

freshly ground pepper

1 tbsp padano (parmesan)

Toss all together.

Served on a bed of lettuce and cucumbers.

SERVES 2 FOR LUNCH.

Yummy Cheese Enchiladas

We have a low-fat menu at the Lazy Gourmet called "café smart" and this is my favourite item from that menu. They're quick and easy to make.

16 6-inch (15 cm) corn tortillas	Wrap tortillas in foil and heat in 350° oven for 10 minutes, or until very pliable.
2 cups (500 mL) ricotta cheese 4 green onions, chopped 4 tsp (20 mL) lemon juice 1 tsp (5 mL) ground coriander ½ tsp (2 mL) cumin ½ tsp (2 mL) chili powder ¼ tsp (1 mL) cayenne	Mix all ingredients together.
	Assemble enchiladas with 2 tbsp (25 mL) cheese and onion mixture in centre of tortilla. Fold in half. Place enchiladas in lightly oiled pan. Cover with foil and bake for 20 minutes at 350°F (180°C). Sprinkle with 2 cups (500 mL) low-fat cheese (mozzarella, Swiss, or Monterey Jack). Bake an additional 4 minutes. Serve with Lazy Gourmet Salsa (see page 232) and plain yogurt. MAKES 16 TORTILLAS.

Cheese and Tomato Kugel

Simple and low in fat, this kugel is very tasty and satisfying.

16 oz (500 g) or 12 oz (375 g) fresh linguine or fettucine	Cook according to package directions. Set aside.
2 tbsp (25 mL) olive oil 2 medium onions, chopped 6 cloves garlic, minced	Sauté onion and garlic in oil until soft. Transfer to large bowl.
½ cup (125 mL) fresh parsley, chopped 1 tbsp (15 mL) dried oregano 2 tbsp (25 mL) lemon juice 2 tsp (10 mL) dried basil ½ tsp (2 mL) pepper	Add to onions and garlic. When thoroughly mixed, toss with pasta.
1 cup (250 mL) ricotta cheese 4 tbsp (60 mL) grated Parmesan cheese 2 egg whites	Combine and toss with pasta.
4 medium tomatoes, peeled, seeded, and chopped ½ cup (125 mL) shredded low-fat cheese	Add to pasta and pour into springform pan.
4 tbsp (60 mL) grated Parmesan cheese	Sprinkle over pasta mixture and bake, covered with foil, at 375°F (190°C) for 40 minutes. Uncover and bake 5 minutes longer.
	Serves 8.

Cauliflower, Broccoli, and Cheddar Kugel

Cauliflower and broccoli are excellent sources of folate. This dish makes a great main course. Start with Papaya Yogurt Soup and fresh rolls and finish with oatmeal cookies for dessert.

12 oz (300 g) egg noodles	Cook according to package instructions. Set aside.
3 tbsp (50 mL) vegetable oil 1 large onion, chopped 2 cloves garlic, minced	Sauté onion and garlic in oil until tender.
½ lb (250 g) mushrooms, sliced	Add to onions and garlic and sauté for 2 minutes, or until soft.
3 cups (750 mL) broccoli florets 3 cups (750 mL) coarsely chopped cauliflower	Microwave broccoli and cauliflower with ¼ cup water on High for 2 minutes, then add to mushroom mixture.
1 cup (250 mL) low-fat plain yogurt 1 cup (250 mL) low-fat cottage cheese 6 oz (150 g) Cheddar cheese, grated 3 eggs, beaten 2 tsp (10 mL) fresh basil, chopped or 1 tsp (5 mL) dried basil 1 tsp (5 mL) dried mustard	Combine in separate bowl.
	Combine noodles, broccoli and cauliflower mixture, and yogurt mixture. Pour into 9 x 13-inch (3.5 L) or bundt pan. Bake at 350°, 35 to 40 minutes until golden on top. SERVES 6 AS A MAIN COURSE AND 8 TO 10 AS A SIDE DISH.

Microwave Mushroom and Green Pea Risotto

This recipe is much easier to make than traditional risotto, which demands that you stand over a stove and stir for 25 minutes. It's every bit as delicious, though.

½ cup (125 mL) chopped onion 2 cloves garlic, minced 2 tsp (10 mL) olive oil	Mix in a 2 qt (2 L) casserole, and microwave 1 minute on High.
6 oz (150 g) uncooked arborio rice (short-grain rice)	Add to onion mixture and microwave for 30 seconds longer.
3½ cups (875 mL) water or vegetable broth 1 cup (250 mL) sliced mushrooms 1 cup (250 mL) frozen peas 4 sun-dried tomatoes, sliced	Add to rice mixture, cover, and microwave on High for 15 minutes, stirring every 2 minutes, until rice is tender and liquid is absorbed.
3 tbsp (50 mL) grated Parmesan cheese 1 tbsp (15 mL) butter	Stir into rice mixture.
	SERVES 4.

Spinach Orzo

Even our mother Roz, who shudders at the thought of spinach, loves this recipe and has been known to ask for seconds!

2 qts (2 L) water 2 cups (500 mL) orzo	Boil orzo in water for about 8 minutes or until tender. Set aside.
1 onion, chopped 3 cloves garlic, minced 4 tsp (20 mL) olive oil	Sauté onion and garlic in oil in large saucepan.
1 bunch spinach	Wash spinach and cook until it is completely wilted (it will be a little watery from the steam). Process in blender until smooth.
4 to 6 tbsp (60 to 100 mL) grated Parmesan cheese Salt and pepper to taste	Toss Parmesan with spinach and orzo. Season with salt and pepper.
	SERVES 6 TO 8.

Broccoli Soufflé

You can never have too many broccoli recipes. Broccoli is probably the all-time winner in nutrients. It is high in calcium, beta-carotene, folate, and fibre.

3 cups (750 mL) broccoli florets	Steam broccoli for 5 minutes. Place in greased 8 x 12-inch (3.5 L) casserole.
1 small onion, chopped 3 tbsp (50 mL) butter	Sauté onion in butter until soft.
2 tbsp (25 mL) flour	Add to onion and stir for one minute.
½ cup (125 mL) water Salt and pepper to taste	Slowly add to onion mixture and cook until thickened, stirring constantly.
3 eggs, beaten 2 cups (500 mL) grated Cheddar cheese	Add to onion mixture.
	Pour onion mixture over broccoli in casserole and bake at 350°F (180°C) for 40 minutes, or until firm in centre. SERVES 6 TO 8.

Easy Broccoli and Tofu Sauté

This recipe offers a good combination of textures and is easy to make, and extremely tasty.

1 tbsp (15 mL) vegetable oil	Heat in nonstick skillet.
2 cloves garlic, minced 1 tbsp (15 mL) grated gingerroot	Add to oil and sauté for 2 minutes, or until soft.
2 cups (500 mL) broccoli florets	Microwave for 2 minutes on High with ¼ cup water and add to ginger and garlic.
2 cups (500 mL) bean sprouts 1 cup (250 mL) sliced carrots	Add to broccoli mixture, sauté 1 minute.
¾ cup (175 mL) vegetable broth 2 tbsp (25 mL) low-sodium soy sauce 2 tbsp (25 mL) rice vinegar 1 tsp (5 mL) cornstarch 1 tsp (5 mL) Japanese sesame oil	Combine and stir to dissolve cornstarch. Add to broccoli mixture and cook 1 minute, or until tender.
¾ lb (375 g) firm tofu, cubed ½ cup (125 mL) celery, sliced on diagonal ½ cup (125 mL) green onions, sliced on diagonal	Add to broccoli mixture, cover, and cook for 1 minute.
	Serve with rice or pasta. SERVES 4 TO 6.

Easy Vegetarian Chili

A delicious way to pump up the fibre. Add Spinach, Romaine, and Strawberry Salad (p. 79) as well as Polenta (p. 98) or Cornbread (p. 229) for a complete meal.

1 cup (250 mL) chopped onions 3 cloves garlic, minced 2 tbsp (25 mL) vegetable oil	Sauté onion and garlic in oil until softened.
1 red pepper, chopped 1 yellow pepper, chopped 1 green pepper, chopped	Add to onion and sauté for 3 minutes.
1 lb (500 g) pressed tofu, chopped into pieces	Add to pepper mixture and cook until browned.
1 28 oz (796 mL) can crushed tomatoes 1 5½-oz (156 mL) can tomato paste 3 tbsp (50 mL) chili powder 1 tbsp (15 mL) dried oregano 1 tsp (5 mL) salt ¼ tsp (1 mL) cayenne ¼ tsp (1 mL) freshly ground pepper	Add to tofu and pepper mixture. Bring to a boil. Reduce and simmer 30 minutes.
1 19-oz (540 mL) can kidney beans, drained 1 19-oz (540 mL) can pinto beans, drained 2 cups (500 mL) frozen corn	Add and simmer an additional 30 minutes.
	SERVES 8 TO 10.

Polenta

Polenta is quick and easy to make and chock full of fibre and starch. It's perfect for family meals or for entertaining.

4 cups (1 L) water	Bring water to a boil in 2 qt (2 L) saucepan.
4 oz (100 g) yellow cornmeal	Stir in cornmeal and cook 5 to 6 minutes, stirring constantly. Remove from heat.
4 oz (100 g) Cheddar cheese, grated 1 tbsp (15 mL) margarine	Add cheese and margarine to cornmeal. Spray 15 x 10-inch (2 L) jelly roll pan with nonstick spray. Pour in cornmeal mixture. Let stand 15 to 20 minutes.
2 tsp (10 mL) olive oil	Baste cornmeal with oil and bake at 450°F (230°C) for about 15 minutes, or until golden. Let cool slightly and cut squares.
	MAKES ABOUT 20 SQUARES.

Eggplant-Tomato Gratin

The key to this recipe is to bake the eggplant until it is soft. To me there's nothing worse than undercooked eggplant!

2 eggplants 2 to 3 tbsp oil	Cut eggplant lengthwise, prick skin with fork. Place cut sides down on baking sheet. Baste with oil. Bake at 450°F (230°C) for 20 minutes or until tender. Let cool, then cut crosswise into ½-inch (1 cm) thick slices. Set aside.
1 28-oz (796 mL) can plum tomatoes, not drained ¼ cup (50 mL) tomato paste 1 onion, finely chopped 1 tbsp (15 mL) dried basil 1 tsp (5 mL) oregano 2 cloves garlic, minced	Purée tomatoes, tomato paste, onion, and herbs in food processor. Pour into heavy pan.
1 large bay leaf	Add bay leaf to tomato mixture. Simmer uncovered for 20 to 30 minutes.
Freshly ground pepper	Season with pepper to taste. Remove bay leaf. Spread thin layer of tomato mixture in a 9 x 13-inch baking dish, cover with layer of eggplant. Continue to layer tomato mixture and eggplant until all have been used up.
1 cup (250 mL) shredded part-skim mozzarella 2 tbsp (25 mL) grated Parmesan cheese	Top casserole with cheeses.
	Bake at 400°F (200°C) for 25 to 30 minutes or until bubbly. SERVES 6 TO 8.

Roasted Potatoes
with Rosemary

This is a garlic lover's dream come true. Feel free to experiment with different herbs. The garlic gets quite crispy, along with the potatoes. Make this recipe a day before you need it, since the flavours blend together wonderfully over 24 hours.

24 small nugget red potatoes, with skin	Cook potatoes in boiling water about 15 minutes, or until tender. Drain and cool. Cover and refrigerate at least 1 hour. Cut potatoes in quarters and put in large roasting pan.
⅓ cup (75 mL) olive oil 2 tbsp (25 mL) chopped fresh rosemary 12 cloves garlic, minced Salt and pepper to taste	Mix together and toss with potatoes.
	Bake at 375°F (190°C), tossing occasionally, for 45 minutes to 1 hour, or until golden and crisp. SERVES 6.

Simple Broccoli Noodles

Serve hot or cold for a quick nutritious lunch or dinner on the run.

4 oz (100 g) spaghettini	Cook in 4 cups (1 L) water until tender (about 12 minutes).
2 broccoli stalks, cut into florets	Add to spaghettini for last 3 minutes of cooking time. Cook until tender. Remove from heat and drain.
1 to 2 tbsp (15 to 25 mL) sesame oil 4 tsp (20 mL) low-sodium soy sauce 1 tbsp (15 mL) balsamic vinegar 2 green onions, chopped	Mix together, then toss with spaghettini and broccoli.
	SERVES 2.

Linguine with Spicy Tomato and Clam Sauce

This recipe is packed with nutrients and is very satisfying. You can substitute mussels for the clams.

1 28-oz (796 mL) can Italian plum tomatoes	Drain in sieve. Chop into small pieces. Set aside.
2 tbsp (25 mL) olive oil	Heat oil in large skillet.
½ red onion, chopped	Sauté onion in oil until tender.
3 cloves garlic, minced 1 tsp (5 mL) chili garlic sauce or ¼ tsp (1 mL) crushed red peppers (optional)	Add to onion and stir for 10 seconds. Add tomatoes to onion mixture.
Salt and pepper to taste 2 tbsp (25 mL) fresh parsley, chopped 1 tbsp (15 mL) fresh marjoram, chopped	Add seasonings to tomato mixture and simmer until thick (about 15 minutes).
1 lb (500 g) clams, scrubbed	Add clams to tomato mixture and cover. Simmer 5 minutes, or until clams have opened. Discard any unopened clams.
½ lb (250 g) linguine	Cook pasta in boiling water until al dente. (Fresh pasta takes 7 to 8 minutes, dried pasta takes 10 to 12 minutes.) Toss sauce, clams, and linguine together, and divide into 2 bowls.
	SERVES 2 HEARTY APPETITES.

Pasta with Sun-dried Tomatoes

This is our favourite pasta dish.

4 cups cooked pasta	Set aside.
½ cup sun-dried tomatoes 2 cups boiling water	Soak in water then cut into small pieces. Save water.
1 large onion 1 tbsp oil 2 cloves garlic	Chop and fry in small batches until dark brown. Add tomatoes and sauté.
1 chili pepper, cut into small pieces (optional)	Add.
4 cups total snow peas, broccoli, asparagus 4 tbsp Parmesan cheese	Steam and add to tomato water and toss with pasta. Add a little pepper. Sprinkle with Parmesan cheese.
	SERVES 2 TO 4.

Linguine with Black Bean Sauce

This recipe was given to me by a chef specializing in fusion food or "East Meets West" cuisine. Everyone in my family loves it.

1 ½ tsp oil 1 small onion, diced fine	Sauté until soft.
2 tbsp ginger, grated 4–6 cloves garlic, minced 1 ½ tsp sesame oil	Add.
1 cup fermented black beans soaked in boiling water 5 minutes and rinsed twice.	Process in food processor. Add to above and stir. Add a little water if you want it a bit smoother.
1 tbsp sugar ½ cup mushroom soy sauce ¼ cup oyster sauce, no msg ¼ cup water	Mix until smooth. Cook 3 minutes.
1 ½ lbs linguine, cooked until al dente 2 cups broccoli flowers, blanched ½ cup thinly sliced red pepper	Toss all ingredients together and serve hot.
	Add 1 tbsp jalapeño peppers if a spicy flavour is preferred.

Carrot and Sweet Potato Tzimmis

This is a great accompaniment for a meat or chicken dish, full of beta-carotene and fibre. I usually serve it for the Jewish New Year as it is sweet and everyone loves it.

2 lbs (1 kg) carrots, chopped 2 lbs (1 kg) sweet potatoes, peeled and cut into chunks	Cook carrots and potatoes in boiling water until tender. Set aside.
½ lb (250 g) dried prunes ½ lb (250 g) dried apricots	Place in a 9 x 13-inch (3.5 L) greased baking pan with the carrots and sweet potatoes.
1 14-oz (398 mL) can crushed pineapple 3 tbsp (50 mL) honey 3 tbsp (50 mL) melted butter Juice and rind from 2 oranges (optional)	Mix together pineapple, honey, butter, and orange juice and rind. Pour over vegetables and dried fruit. Bake at 350°F (180°C) for 30 minutes, stirring occasionally.
	SERVES 8 TO 10.

Spinach in Phyllo with Sesame Seeds

This is the best way to get my family to eat spinach. Everyone gets an individual packet of spinach. Experiment with different cheeses—some people find the feta too salty.

1 cup (250 mL) chopped onion 3 cloves garlic, minced 2 tbsp (25 mL) olive oil	In large saucepan, sauté onion and garlic in oil until tender.
2 cups (500 mL) sliced mushrooms 1 large bunch spinach, washed and chopped	Add to onions and garlic and sauté until mushrooms are soft and spinach is wilted. Remove from heat.
5 oz (125 g) feta cheese, crumbled 2 eggs, beaten 1/4 cup (50 mL) bread crumbs Pinch nutmeg Salt and pepper to taste	In large bowl, combine cheese, eggs, bread crumbs, and seasonings. Combine with spinach-mushroom mixture.
6 phyllo pastry sheets	Spread out phyllo pastry sheets. Spray with vegetable spray. Place 1/6 of mixture on each sheet. Fold over sides and roll up. Spray and sprinkle with sesame seeds. Bake at 375°F (190°C) for 18 minutes, or until golden.
	SERVES 6.

Triple Bell Pepper and Onion Quesadillas

Quesadillas are fun to make and once you know how, you will have a great time experimenting with different fillings and cheeses. Serve with a salad for a terrific lunch, or serve alone with salsa for a great hors d'oeuvre. Corn tortillas are delicious and have more fibre than flour tortillas.

½ onion, chopped 1 tbsp (15 mL) vegetable oil	Sauté onion in oil until tender.
½ red pepper, chopped finely ½ green pepper, chopped finely ½ yellow pepper, chopped finely	Add and sauté until tender. Set aside.
3 oz (75 g) goat cheese, crumbled 4 oz (100 g) mozzarella cheese, grated	Mix together.
8 6-inch (15 cm) flour tortillas	Fill four tortillas with ¼ of the filling and ¼ of the cheese mixture. Press a second tortilla gently on top of each one.
	Bake at 350°F (180°C) for 12 to 15 minutes, or until tortillas are crispy and the cheese has melted. Cut into triangles and serve with salsa. SERVES 4.

Grandma Faye's Apricot Chicken

A Friday-night favourite of adults and kids in our house. It's an often-requested recipe at the Lazy Gourmet.

4 lb (2 kg) roasting chicken	Cut chicken into serving pieces. Remove skin. Set aside.
1 cup (250 mL) apricot jam ½ cup (125 mL) chili sauce ¼ cup (50 mL) dry white wine 2 tbsp (25 mL) low-sodium soy sauce 2 tbsp (25 mL) honey 1 tbsp (15 mL) grated gingerroot ¼ tsp (1 mL) salt	Combine with a whisk in saucepan. Heat until well blended. Bring to low boil and remove from heat.
	Place chicken in large roasting pan. Baste thoroughly with sauce. Bake at 375°F (190°C) for 50 to 60 minutes, or until chicken is thoroughly cooked. If glaze is not sticky, pour it back into saucepan and cook until reduced and thick. Place chicken on plate and pour sauce on top to glaze. Serve with rice. SERVES 4 TO 8.

Grilled Spicy Peanut Chicken Breasts

An easy last-minute menu for a summer barbecue. It's chock full of flavour and bound to get rave reviews.

6 individual chicken breasts 4 tbsp (60 mL) lime juice 2 tbsp (25 mL) peanut oil	Marinate chicken breasts for 20 minutes in lime juice and oil. Remove chicken. Save marinade.
2/3 cup (150 mL) chicken broth 1/2 cup (125 mL) creamy peanut butter 1 1/2 jalapeño chilis, chopped 2 tbsp (25 mL) grated gingerroot 2 tbsp (25 mL) low-sodium soy sauce 1 tsp (5 mL) sugar 4 cloves garlic, minced	Blend ingredients in food processor. Pour into saucepan, add marinade, and simmer over a low heat for 10 minutes, or until heated through.
	Grill or broil chicken breasts. Pour sauce on top to serve. SERVES 6.

Soy Sesame Chicken with Oriental Vegetables

This chicken recipe can be eaten hot or cold.

6 tbsp (100 mL) low-sodium soy sauce ¼ cup (50 mL) cilantro, chopped ¼ cup (50 mL) chopped green onion ¼ cup (50 mL) chicken or vegetable broth 2 tbsp (25 mL) grated gingerroot 2 tbsp (25 mL) rice wine vinegar 2 tsp (10 mL) hot chili paste with garlic 1 tsp (5 mL) sesame oil 4 cloves garlic, minced	Combine ingredients in bowl. Pour half of marinade into a separate bowl and set aside.
6 4 oz (100 g) boneless, skinless chicken breasts	Cover chicken with one-half of marinade. Refrigerate for 20 minutes.
1½ cups (375 mL) thinly sliced carrots 1½ cups (375 mL) snow peas, cut into threes 1 cup (250 mL) chopped broccoli florets	Cook vegetables with ½ cup water in microwave for 2 minutes on High.
1 tbsp (15 mL) peanut oil	Heat oil in large skillet. Add chicken, smooth side down, and cook for 3 to 4 minutes. Turn and sprinkle with sesame seeds and heat for another 4 to 5 minutes, or until chicken is thoroughly cooked. Add the remainder of marinade and the vegetables, and stir until vegetables are done.
	SERVES 6.

Halibut with Black Bean Sauce

I love to cook with fermented black beans. They can be found in Chinese food stores everywhere. Be sure to soak and rinse them well.

1 cup (250 mL) water 2 to 3 tbsp (25 to 50 mL) Chinese fermented black beans	Soak beans for 10 minutes in cold water, then drain and rinse. Place in small bowl.
3 cloves garlic, minced 2 tbsp (25 mL) low-sodium soy sauce 1 tbsp (15 mL) grated gingerroot 2 tsp (10 mL) sesame oil 2 tsp (10 mL) rice vinegar	Combine ingredients with beans and mash into paste or process in food mill.
1½ lbs (750 g) halibut or snapper fillets	Put rinsed fillets into lightly oiled 9 x 13-inch baking dish. Spread bean paste over fillets. Cover dish with foil.
	Bake at 375°F (190°C) for 20 to 25 minutes, or until fish flakes. Serve with rice and green vegetables. MAKES 4 6-OZ SERVINGS, OR 6 4-OZ SERVINGS.

Swordfish with Apricot Sauce

I often serve this after I've rushed home from work and want an easy and special dinner. This sauce is also great as a last-minute sauce for chicken breasts. I just baste the chicken breasts and put them in a 375°F (190°C) oven for about 35 minutes. I also use this recipe for halibut and snapper.

1½ lbs (750 g) swordfish fillets Juice of ½ lemon	Rinse fillets and sprinkle with lemon juice.
½ cup (125 mL) apricot jam 3 tbsp (50 mL) low-sodium soy sauce 2 tbsp (25 mL) honey	Mix together and brush onto swordfish.
	Place fish under broiler. Broil about 6 minutes on each side. Be careful not to overcook. MAKES 4 6-OZ SERVINGS OR 6 4-OZ SERVINGS.

Sole Rolled and Stuffed with Crab and Shrimp

This is a low-fat variation of a richer recipe that I make. I like it even better than the original.

1 ½ tbsp butter 1 onion, chopped 2 cups sliced mushrooms ½ cup chopped parsley	In frypan, sauté.
3 oz crab 3 oz shrimp	Add.
6 3 oz filets of sole	Fold the sole filets over filling (what would have been skin side up) on a bed of partially steamed spinach with lemon slices on top.
	Bake at 350° for 15 to 20 minutes.

Vegetarian Loaf

I like to keep this around for a light lunch or sustenance to get me through an afternoon. I always feel healthy after I eat it and it's full of protein, fibre, vitamins, and minerals.

1 tbsp (15 mL) peanut oil	Heat in nonstick saucepan.
2 cups (500 mL) grated carrots 2 cups (500 mL) chopped mushrooms 1 cup (250 mL) chopped celery 1 cup (250 mL) chopped red pepper 1 cup (250 mL) chopped onion	Add vegetables and sauté about 5 minutes, or until softened.
2 19 oz (540 mL) cans chickpeas 2 eggs	Combine eggs and chickpeas in food processor until coarsely chopped, and add to vegetables.
½ cup (125 mL) bread crumbs ½ tsp (2 mL) sea salt ¼ tsp (1 mL) pepper ¼ tsp (1 mL) cumin	Add to mixture and stir well.
	Press mixture into nonstick loaf pan sprayed with nonstick cooking spray. Bake at 375°F (190°C) for 30 minutes or until firm to touch. Serve hot or cold with tzatziki. SERVES 6.

Falafel Burgers

These burgers are high in protein and fibre but low in fat. Deep frying is the traditional way of preparing falafel: these are baked.

¾ cup (175 mL) water	Bring to a boil.
2 oz (50 g) uncooked bulgur	Add bulgur to boiling water. Reduce heat to low and simmer for 10 minutes. Remove from heat and let stand 10 more minutes. Drain and transfer to large bowl. Set aside.
½ lb (250 g) cooked chickpeas 2 tsp (10 mL) lemon juice ½ tsp (2 mL) cumin ¼ tsp (1 mL) sea salt ¼ tsp (1 mL) pepper 2 cloves garlic, minced	Process in food processor until smooth. Add to bulgur.
¼ cup (50 mL) bread crumbs	Add to bulgur and mix well.
	Shape mixture into 12 large balls. Arrange on baking sheet sprayed with vegetable spray. Bake at 450°F (230 °C) for 15 minutes, or until lightly browned. Serve with tzatziki or tahini sauce (see pages 213 and 220). MAKES 12 FALAFEL BALLS.

Vegetarian Nut Burgers

This is the hottest-selling burger at the Lazy Gourmet.

3 cups (750 mL) chopped walnuts

2½ cups (625 mL) fine bread crumbs

1 cup (125 mL) grated carrots

⅓ cup (75 mL) grated Monterey Jack cheese

⅓ cup (75 mL) hulled sunflower seeds

4 large eggs

2 tbsp tamari or soy sauce

2 tsp crushed garlic

½ cup vegetable oil

Mix together thoroughly. (A food processor makes this easy.)

Form mixture into patties and grill, turning to brown both sides.

MAKES 8 TO 12 PATTIES.

Lynnie's Couscous

Our sister Lynn often serves this to large crowds and always gets rave reviews.

¼ cup (50 mL) butter 2 medium onions, chopped	Sauté onions in butter until translucent.
1 cup (250 mL) chopped celery 2 tsp (10 mL) ground coriander 2 tsp (10 mL) cinnamon ¼ tsp (1 mL) cayenne ¼ tsp (1 mL) saffron	Add to onion and cook additional 5 minutes.
2 lbs (1 kg) beef, cut into small cubes 2 19-oz (540 mL) cans plum tomatoes 1 14-oz (398 mL) can chickpeas 6 carrots, cut into chunks 4 turnips, cut into chunks 4 small zucchini, cut into chunks 2 acorn squashes, cut into small pieces 2 red peppers, cut into chunks 2 sticks cinnamon, cut into pieces 3 tbsp (50 mL) fresh parsley, chopped	Add to onion and celery mixture and bring to a boil. Simmer for 30 minutes.
2 lbs (1 kg) couscous 8 cups (2 L) boiling salted water	Put couscous in water. Let sit for 5 minutes.
4 tbsp (60 mL) olive oil	Put oil in large skillet and toss with couscous for 5 minutes on Medium heat.
	Serve vegetable and beef mixture on a bed of couscous. SERVES 8.

Spinach and Tofu in Phyllo

This is a complete meal in an envelope.

1 large head spinach	Wash spinach. Microwave 2 minutes on High. Squeeze out excess water and chop. Set aside.
2 tsp (10 mL) vegetable oil	Pour into large skillet.
1 cup (250 mL) chopped onion 2 cloves garlic, minced	Add to oil and cook until translucent.
1 cup (250 mL) chopped red peppers	Add to skillet and sauté 1 minute. Add spinach. Remove from heat.
2 eggs, beaten 3 tbsp (50 mL) grated Parmesan cheese	Mix eggs and cheese together and add to spinach.
½ lb (250 g) tofu, cubed 3 tbsp (50 mL) bread crumbs ½ tsp (2 mL) sea salt ¼ tsp (1 mL) nutmeg ¼ tsp (1 mL) pepper	Add to spinach and stir well.
6 sheets phyllo pastry	Spray each sheet with vegetable spray. Place ⅙ mixture on each sheet. Fold in sides and roll up into either log or envelope shape.
	Bake at 425°F (220°C) for 18 minutes, or until lightly browned. MAKES 6 ENVELOPES.

Tofu Burritos

This combination will provide all four food groups in one dish.

1 ½ lbs (750 g) medium-texture tofu (any tofu will work)	Cut into 3 inch (7 cm) slices. Press excess water out of tofu by putting tofu on wire rack or cookie sheet and covering with flat casserole weighted with 3 or 4 cans. Let sit for 30 minutes. Drain and crumble tofu into bowl.
2 tbsp (25 mL) vegetable oil	Heat oil in large skillet.
2 cups (500 mL) chopped onion 3 cloves garlic, minced	Sauté in oil until tender.
1 or 2 jalapeño peppers, chopped fine 1 red pepper, chopped	Add to onion and garlic and sauté.
1 tsp (5 mL) dried oregano 1 tsp (5 mL) paprika 1 tsp (5 mL) ground coriander ¼ tsp (1 mL) chili powder	Add to peppers and cook for 2 more minutes.
3 tbsp (50 mL) tomato paste 3 tbsp (50 mL) low-sodium soy sauce 1 cup (250 mL) frozen corn, thawed	Add to pepper mixture and stir. Add tofu.
6 10-inch (25 cm) flour tortillas	Spoon ¾ cup (175 mL) filling on centre of each tortilla. Roll up, enclosing filling. Spray 9 x 13-inch baking dish with vegetable spray. Arrange tortillas on dish, seam side down, spray with vegetable spray, and bake at 350°F (180°C) for 20 minutes, or until burritos are heated through. Serve with salsa and yogurt if desired. MAKES 6 TORTILLAS.

Tofu Peanut Fettucine

Serve as a nutritious meal for lunch or dinner.

1 cup (250 mL) broccoli florets ¾ cup (175 mL) thinly sliced carrots	Cook vegetables in glass dish with ¼ cup water in microwave on High for 2 minutes. Set aside.
1 tbsp (15 mL) vegetable oil	Heat in saucepan on High.
1 cup (250 mL) bean sprouts ½ cup (125 mL) thinly sliced red pepper	Add broccoli, carrots, sprouts, and pepper to oil and sauté for 2 minutes.
½ cup (125 mL) chopped green onions	Stir into saucepan.
¾ cup (175 mL) vegetable or chicken broth 3 tbsp (50 mL) creamy peanut butter 4 tsp (20 mL) low-sodium soy sauce 2 tsp (10 mL) brown sugar 1 tsp (5 mL) chili paste 1 tsp (5 mL) cornstarch	Whisk together, then add to vegetable mixture.
½ lb (250 g) tofu, cubed	Add to vegetable mixture, lower heat, cover, and cook 3 to 4 minutes.
3 cups (750 mL) cooked fettucine	Add to vegetable mixture and toss.
½ cup (125 mL) chopped roasted peanuts	Use as a garnish.
	SERVES 3 TO 4.

Tofu with Red Peppers, Broccoli, and Snow Peas

This recipe takes minutes to prepare, and is very colourful, satisfying and nutritious.

2 tbsp (25 mL) peanut oil	Pour into wok, heat, and swirl around.
2 cloves garlic, minced 1 tbsp minced gingerroot	Add to oil and cook 1 minute.
8 oz tofu, cut into small squares 1 tbsp (15 mL) sake 1 tsp (5 mL) low-sodium soy sauce 1/4 tsp (1 mL) garlic powder	Toss tofu with sake, soy sauce, and garlic and add to wok. Sauté until lightly browned. Remove to serving platter. Cover to keep warm.
1 cup (250 mL) broccoli florets 1 small onion, chopped 1/2 red pepper, chopped 1/2 cup (125 mL) snow peas	Put broccoli, onion, and pepper into wok and sauté until broccoli is bright green. Add snow peas at the last minute. Return tofu to wok.
2 tbsp (25 mL) low-sodium soy sauce 1 tbsp (15 mL) sake 2 tsp (10 mL) vegetable stock	Add to wok and simmer 1 more minute.
	Serve hot over steamed rice. SERVES 2 TO 4 DEPENDING ON APPETITE OR 2 DINNER, 4 LUNCH PORTIONS.

Vegetable Fried Rice with Tofu

A meal in itself.

1 cup (250 mL) chopped onion 1 tbsp (15 mL) grated gingerroot 2 cloves garlic, minced 2 tbsp (25 mL) peanut oil	Sauté in wok or skillet onions, ginger, and garlic in oil.
1 cup (250 mL) chopped red cabbage 1 cup (250 mL) thinly sliced carrots 1 cup (250 mL) thinly sliced red peppers	Add and cook until cabbage softens.
3 cups (750 mL) cooked basmati rice	Add to cabbage mixture.
3 tbsp (50 mL) low-sodium soy sauce ¼ cup (50 mL) vegetable broth 1 tbsp (15 mL) sherry 1 tsp (5 mL) brown sugar ½ tsp (2 mL) chili paste ½ tsp (2 mL) sesame oil	Combine and add to cabbage and rice mixture.
¾ cup (175 mL) frozen peas	Heat peas for 1 minute in microwave on High. Then add to cabbage and rice mixture.
½ lb (250 g) tofu, cubed	Add to cabbage and rice mixture and heat until tofu is hot.
1 to 2 eggs (optional) 1 tsp (5 mL) vegetable oil (optional)	Quick fry eggs in oil in a skillet and add to tofu mixture.
	Serves 4.

Apple Strudel

I make these in mini triangle versions for variety. The idea was stolen from a dessert served at a health spa in Arizona.

3 apples	Peel, core and slice and set aside.
5 tbsp brown sugar 1 tsp cinnamon	Mix well together and set aside.
6 sheets phyllo vegetable spray	Assembly: Lay out one sheet of phyllo. Spray with vegetable spray for 1 second. Place ½ sliced apple along edge of phyllo. Sprinkle with ⅙ sugar mixture and fold over edges. Now roll up completely. Spray with vegetable spray. Bake 400° for 12-15 minutes until golden.

Blueberry Strudel Variation

3 cups blueberries 6 tbsp sugar 1 tbsp cornstarch	Proceed according to above instructions with this blueberry filling.

Triple Berry Crisp

Take advantage of seasonal fruits to experiment with different variations on this recipe. This recipe started with raspberries, blueberries, and strawberries—but we thought the peaches added more flavour! We kept the original name.

2 cups (500 mL) sliced peaches 2 cups (500 mL) fresh or frozen raspberries 2 cups (500 mL) fresh or frozen blueberries ½ cup (125 mL) sugar 3 tbsp (50 mL) cornstarch ¼ tsp (1 mL) nutmeg	Mix together in large bowl and turn into 9-inch (23 cm) pie plate. Set aside.
1 cup (250 mL) quick-cooking oats ½ cup (125 mL) brown sugar ¾ cup (175 mL) flour 5 tbsp (75 mL) cold butter	Rub together to form crumb topping. Spread over berries.
	Place pie pan on cookie sheet (to catch extra juice) and bake at 375°F (190°C) for 40 minutes. MAKES 6 SERVINGS.

Honey Biscotti

This is a wonderful low-fat snack. The traditional biscotti are extremely crunchy, so be forewarned. I especially like them because each cookie takes about 10 minutes to eat! This is not a cookie for kids.

Ingredients	Instructions
1 ¼ cup (50 mL) whole almonds	Toast almonds for 10 minutes in 375° oven and set aside.
3 large eggs, beaten ½ cup (125 mL) honey 1 tsp (5 mL) vanilla ½ tsp (2 mL) licorice flavouring	Combine and mix well. Set aside.
3 cups (750 mL) unbleached flour ½ cup (125 mL) sugar 1 tsp (5 mL) baking powder ½ tsp (2 mL) white pepper ½ tsp (2 mL) ground ginger ¼ tsp (1 mL) salt	Sift dry ingredients together. Add egg mixture all at once. Beat with electric beater on low speed until dough holds together. Fold in almonds.
	Lightly flour a large work surface and turn dough out onto the floured area. Sift ¼ cup flour over top of dough. Shape into 3 logs. Bake 50 minutes at 300°F (150°C), then slice into diagonals. Place cookies cut side down on cookie sheet, reduce oven heat to 275°F (140°C) and bake for 20 minutes. Turn over and bake another 20 minutes. MAKES 3 DOZEN BISCOTTI.

Meringues

A low-fat snack for sweet cravings!

3 egg whites	Beat until stiff, but not dry.
1 cup (250 mL) sugar	Add very gradually to eggs. Beat for 10 minutes, or until very thick.
¾ cup (175 mL) long threaded coconut ¼ tsp (1 mL) vanilla ¼ cup (50 mL) chopped pecans (optional)	Combine and fold into beaten eggs.
	Drop spoonfuls of the mixture onto waxed-paper–covered cookie sheet. Bake at 350°F (180°C) for 25 to 30 minutes, or until lightly golden. MAKES 3 DOZEN.

Raspberry Coulis

*Serve as a sauce for ice milk, yogurt, and other fruits. For an
unusual peach melba, smother a peeled peach with plain yogurt
and top with raspberry coulis.*

2 cups (500 mL) fresh or frozen raspberries ¼ cup (50 mL) sugar	Combine berries and sugar in saucepan. Simmer over low heat for 2 minutes, or until raspberries are softened. Stir constantly to prevent burning.
2 tsp (10 mL) cornstarch 2 tbsp (25 mL) cold water	Dissolve cornstarch in water. Add to berries and stir for about 30 seconds, or until fruit is translucent. Strain through a fine sieve, pressing to extract as much pulp as possible. Cool. MAKES 1½ CUPS OF COULIS.

Peach Shortcake

A hearty dessert with little fat and lots of summer flavour. I adapted this recipe from a much richer recipe with sour cream. Everyone actually likes this one better!

1 ½ cups (375 mL) flour 1 tbsp (15 mL) baking powder 1 tsp (5 mL) baking soda	Sift together dry ingredients.
½ cup (125 mL) brown sugar Pinch salt	Add to flour mixture.
⅓ cup (75 mL) shortening	Cut into flour mixture.
1 egg, beaten ¾ cup (175 mL) 2% milk	Combine eggs and milk and add to flour mixture, which will become a stiff batter.
½ cup (125 mL) chopped pecans (optional)	Add to batter. Bake in 9-inch round pan at 375°F (190°C) for 25 minutes. Cool, then cut horizontally. Set aside to cool.
2 cups (500 mL) plain low-fat yogurt ⅓ to ½ cup (75 to 125 mL) brown sugar	Mix together yogurt and sugar. Set aside.
4 cups (1 L) peaches, peeled, pitted, and sliced	Place one layer of cake on plate. Spread with yogurt mixture and top with peaches. Add second layer of cake, another layer of yogurt mixture, and top with peaches.
	SERVES 8.

Pavlova

Attractive, delicious, and nutritious.

3 egg whites	Beat eggs until stiff, but not dry.
⅔ cup (150 mL) sugar	Gradually add sugar to eggs and beat for 10 minutes, or until thick.
½ tsp (2 mL) vanilla	Fold into eggs.
Parchment paper	Cut paper into 10 circles. Place on cookie sheet and cover with egg mixture. Shape into cups using back of spoon. Bake at 275°F (140°C) for 25 minutes or until lightly golden. Set aside to cool.
2 cups (500 mL) yogurt or frozen yogurt, any flavour	Fill meringue cups with yogurt.
2 cups (500 mL) strawberries, blueberries, raspberries, kiwi, banana, etc.	Top yogurt with fresh fruit.
	SERVES 8.

PART TWO

INFANCY

THE FIRST YEAR OF LIFE IS A REMARKABLE TIME FOR parents as well as the new member of the human race. Your newborn arrives with little more than the capacity to be fed, but by the time her first birthday is celebrated, she can manipulate a wide range of foods—as well as people. This section provides the information you need to think about even before the baby arrives. Whether you choose to breastfeed or bottle feed, this chapter will answer some of your questions. We also discuss introducing baby's first foods and the delight of finger foods. There are guidelines to follow and suggestions on how to manage the whole food adventure. In addition, we have provided some creative recipes to tempt the most discerning young gourmets.

It's a Baby!

When your baby arrives, you will be so absorbed in the challenges of parenting that you won't have much time for decision making. The time to think about how you want to feed your baby is when you are still pregnant. The first decision has to do with breastfeeding vs bottle feeding. Later, you will have to make other decisions about family eating patterns and the role food plays in the life of your child. Most of these decisions will depend on the attitudes to food you have developed through personal experiences. People who grow up with healthy attitudes towards food and body image will pass this gift on to their children by their own example and by their response to their children's eating patterns. People who grow up with fears about food and body image may recreate these harmful attitudes and behaviours in their children. If they perceive themselves as overweight, they may restrict their child's food intake, or deny them certain foods they consider to be fattening. There are a few examples in the pediatric journals about mothers with a history of anorexia who underfeed their children, causing growth retardation. On the other hand, parents with childhood memories of others teasing them for being skinny or small may try to overfeed their children to encourage growth. In either case, parents run the risk of creating unnecessary food issues with their kids. If you have had difficulties with eating disorders or body image yourself, it might be harder for you to pass on a healthy attitude towards eating to your children. We hope this book will provide some guidelines, but you might want to consider visiting a dietitian or counsellor to overcome these difficulties.

Whatever your early experiences may have been, you need to understand the different effects that food can have on your child's growth, development, and behaviour. You will probably find yourself discussing your questions in great detail with other new parents and with doctors, friends, and relatives. These include questions about the most basic infant feeding and caring issues, from breastfeeding to diapers and from sleeping arrangements to the latest infant music recordings. The purpose of this chapter is to give parents an understanding of the feeding issues relevant to the first year of life. The next chapter will focus on feeding children who can feed themselves.

Breastfeeding vs Bottle Feeding

The human race has survived because of breast milk. But although breastfeeding is a natural, healthy way to feed your child, there are now a few generations which have been successfully fed by formulas based on milk. Until safe formulas were available, breast milk was the only reliable way to feed new babies and ensure their survival. In earlier times, wet nurses were chosen to feed babies for mothers who were unable or unwilling to breastfeed. These substitute breastfeeders were women who had recently had their own babies or women who had never stopped producing breast milk after their last baby was born. The selection of the wet nurse was often based on the woman's personal qualities, because people believed that human characteristics were passed on through the breast milk and that a wise woman could pass her wisdom on to the new child.

Today, with all of the effective formulas on the market, there is not much call for wet nurses. If a mother is unable or unwilling to breastfeed, she can opt for one of the many formulas now available and be assured that her child will thrive. Through the 1970s and 1980s, however, the Hospital for Sick Children in Toronto maintained a breast milk bank for babies who needed human milk for one reason or another. But during the 1980s, a flurry of research activity led to increased knowledge about the composition of breast milk as well as the capacity to manufacture some (but not all) of those components.

During the 1960s, the "return to nature" movement set the stage for a resurgence in breastfeeding, to counteract the move to so-called "scientific" infant feeding that began in the 1950s. At that time, the popular notion was that scientists could outdo Mother Nature. During the 1970s political activism and a spate of deaths of bottle-fed babies in the less-developed countries created a new emphasis on the importance of breastfeeding. Television, magazines, and books reinforced the virtues of breastfeeding. Health care professionals joined the bandwagon and before long, breastfeeding became the norm. As a result, the number of breastfeeding mothers in most of the higher-income nations rose consistently and reached a peak in 1984, but for some curious reason, has been gradually falling ever since.

In parts of Canada, the numbers have remained quite high relative to other parts of the world. However, many advocates of breastfeeding are wondering what might account for the decline of breastfeeding in countries such as the United States, Britain, and Australia. One explanation may be related to some of the problems women experience in their efforts to breastfeed. Even though members of every other species manage to feed their babies without trained instructors, humans simply are not born with this knowledge. Nor do women in industrialized countries regularly see others breastfeeding successfully which would help them mimic the behaviour. During her hospital stay, a new mother needs clear information as well as reassurance and support to help her feed her baby properly. Breastfeeding may also be hindered by certain hospital procedures. Hospital staff sometimes feed babies with formula, believing that they are giving the mother a rest. What they may be doing is interfering with the baby's appetite and the breasts' natural response to demand.

With hospital stays growing ever shorter, your access to a nursing instructor will be limited and any problems that develop at home will require someone else with knowledge and a supportive attitude. Your obstetrician is mainly interested in the delivery and anything related to its success or failure. Your pediatrician is mainly interested in the baby. Unless you are seeing a woman doctor who has also breastfed, your family physician may not be intimately familiar with breastfeeding problems. What you need is ready access to a professional, friend, or relative with the experience, knowledge, and time to help you through the first few weeks. A good book on breastfeeding is also essential to help answer your questions.

There are many advantages to breastfeeding which outweigh some of the problems. Breastfeeding reduces the chances that babies will suffer from allergic reactions, since babies are seldom allergic to their mother's milk. Breast milk is very convenient and economical. It requires no preparation or sterilization, and is always ready to serve. The only cost is the extra food required to feed the mother so that she has the energy demanded for milk production. Some of this energy comes from the extra fat that is naturally stored during pregnancy for this purpose. Many women might see this as a real advantage: eat more and lose weight at the same time! There are also a number of irreplaceable ingredients in breast milk; these include the mother's antibodies which offer protection against illness during the first few months, as well as hormones and certain fats that encourage healthy growth and development. Even though scientists have been able to identify and measure most of these components, the only way of giving all of them to babies is through the cheapest food on the market: breast milk.

Researchers have also investigated the role of breastfeeding in terms of the protection it may offer women against cancer and osteoporosis in later life. It may also protect babies against ear infection, respiratory disease, obesity and diabetes. Although this research is not yet conclusive, it is clear that breastfeeding has many advantages.

Women need to know about some of the problems they may encounter with breastfeeding. These include engorged breasts, cracked nipples, and infections inside the breast tissue. Infections require medical intervention, but most women are advised to continue breastfeeding. As for the other problems, you can continue to breastfeed with knowledge, support, and help. Women may also switch to bottle feeding because they are worried that the baby isn't getting enough sustenance, because they find breastfeeding too exhausting, or because there is no one else to feed the baby when they are not available. As long as the baby continues to grow and has 6–8 wet diapers per day, you can have some assurance that the baby is getting enough milk.

Although both breastfed and bottle-fed babies grow well in length, weight, and head circumference in the first six months, recent evidence suggests that formula-fed babies grow faster. This has sparked great debates about the merits of bottle feeding, and formula companies promote this information whenever possible.

But there is a key question that has not yet been answered to anyone's satisfaction: is faster growth advantageous or harmful in the long run?

Ultimately, the decision to breastfeed or bottle feed is a personal one and no woman should be made to feel that she has made an error in judgement. Your key concern should be to learn the proper techniques of infant feeding, whatever method you choose.

Breastfeeding

You should start breastfeeding as soon as possible after your baby is born. Although your baby has practised sucking and swallowing even before delivery, you need to learn how to provide milk. This may require some instruction and practice.

During the first few days of life, mature milk has not yet formed. Instead, the baby receives colostrum, a thin yellowish liquid loaded with antibodies and nutrients that protect the baby during the first days of life. Between the second and fifth day after delivery, your breasts will suddenly feel quite full and may hurt because of the production of mature milk taking place at this time.

A fascinating aspect of breastfeeding is that the production of milk responds directly to the baby's demands. The more the baby suckles, the more milk is produced. If only all our demands were so easily accommodated! This is why it is important to continue to breastfeed the infant on a regular basis to ensure that milk production develops into an established pattern. This principle also supports the decision to breastfeed on demand. For most mothers and for their babies, it is easier to feed when the baby appears to be hungry. However, this can be a difficult call, because babies cry for a variety of reasons; hunger is not the only one. They may cry because they want comfort, warmth, or a change of diaper, or simply because they are feeling fussy. They may also cry if they need burping. This sort of cry may accompany the strange behaviour of pulling away from the bottle or breast even while they are trying to feed. (Babies need regular burping, regardless of the type of feeding selected.) It is amazing how quickly most mothers learn to distinguish the cry for food from other sounds.

Setting up a feeding pattern takes at least the first few weeks of life and may take as long as three months. Most babies will settle into a feeding pattern of about every two and a half to three hours in six weeks or so. As your baby nurses, your breasts will respond by producing milk. Gradually you will both adjust, but just when you think you have figured out a workable routine, things begin to change. Perhaps it is a return to work or other responsibilities that require some adaptation. Whatever the reason, you'll find yourself making continual adjustments from now on.

Feeding the Nursing Mother

Nutrition is just as important when you are breastfeeding as it is when you are pregnant. In fact, now you really are eating for two and your nutritional requirements are even higher than they were during pregnancy. Good nutrition will ensure that you produce adequate milk and that you protect your own body stores throughout this time. To meet your own needs and those of your baby, you should make every effort to get nourishing food, plenty of rest, and emotional support. Relaxed and healthy mothers provide the best start for happy, healthy babies.

Breastfed babies have fewer digestive problems, but many women blame themselves for any problems their babies have during nursing, such as diarrhea, gas, rashes, or fever. You shouldn't have to eliminate any of the food groups from your own diet to combat any of the baby's feeding problems. However some women are advised to stop eating vegetables in order to reduce gas. Other women may be advised not to drink milk or eat cheese to reduce colic in the baby. Unless there is a very good reason for eliminating a particular food, this approach could cause nutritional problems for you later on.

For example, restricting dairy products during nursing may cause problems when you are older. This is because it takes a lot of calcium to make breast milk. If your diet does not provide calcium, a supplement would be in order. This situation is aggravated if the time between weaning one baby and starting another pregnancy is short. Frequent pregnancies, with long periods of breastfeeding, place such a high demand on the mother for calcium that unless you are getting plenty of calcium and vitamin D in your diet, your bones will be the source of the baby's calcium.

At present, nutrient supplements are not routinely recommended for nursing mothers unless there is a specific reason. Teenagers and strict vegetarians may need them, as well as women who have to avoid dairy products because of lactose intolerance or women who have special dietary restrictions.

Almost any variety of food in the diet will give you the energy you need for milk production. However, the nutrients in your diet must be high enough to supply your milk with nutrients and spare your body stores. Therefore, the use of a vitamin mineral supplement during this period of time should be considered in the same way as during pregnancy.

The food you eat will not strongly affect the nutrient levels in your milk but instead will affect the flavour and composition of the milk. For example, the level of fatty acids in the milk will reflect the mother's own intake and may also reflect her own body fat if she is losing weight. If she eats lots of butter, beef, and cheese, her milk will be higher in saturated fats. If she eats mainly vegetable oils, grains, and cereals, her milk will be higher in unsaturated fats. Dairy farmers have known about this effect for years!

If you are breastfeeding your baby, you will produce about 30 to 35 fluid oz (850 mL to 1 L) of milk a day, which costs an extra 1000 calories a day. Your need for energy is now higher than it was when you were pregnant. Some of the extra calories may be provided by the fat that your body stored during pregnancy. During breastfeeding, you may lose a pound (0.45 kg) a week, or you may find that your weight does not begin to drop until after you have finished breastfeeding, because the increased volume of breast tissue keeps your body weight a little higher than normal. Throughout this time you should continue to eat to appetite.

As much as a quart (1 L) of fluid is lost each day through the breast milk. To supply the fluid for milk, you'll need plenty of water and other liquids. Have water, juice, or milk on hand at all times.

All mothers may need extra iron if they lost a lot of blood during delivery. It may be necessary to take a supplement until your body stores have recovered. As long as you are not menstruating, your need for iron will return to the level before pregnancy. Although breastfeeding may stop menstruation for several months, this is not a signal to stop using birth control.

Special Concerns

Breastfeeding and exercise

During the first three months after the baby has arrived, you may feel an exhaustion that cannot be explained by lack of sleep alone. Fatigue may be partly the result of the continuous production of milk, which demands a lot of energy from your body. For this reason, you should set reasonable goals for yourself so that you don't overextend your resources. You need to recover from childbirth, to care for the newborn, and to support breastfeeding.

Within a few weeks or months, depending on your lifestyle, you may be keen to return to some sort of exercise. Studies have not shown any major effect of exercise on milk volume or composition. However, after a heavy workout, your milk will contain higher levels of lactic acid, possibly giving it a sour taste. If your baby does not nurse well after you have been exercising, consider reducing the intensity of exercise or give the baby formula for the first feeding after a workout. You and your baby may be more comfortable if you nurse before exercise. That way you can enjoy the exercise and the baby can enjoy the meal.

Combining breastfeeding and bottle feeding

The decision to breastfeed doesn't mean that you will never use a bottle. You may need more than two hours off once in a while. If you plan to use bottles occasionally, introduce one before the baby reaches four to six weeks. This will ensure that he will accept one in an emergency situation. If the mother requires a regular time away from the baby, give him a bottle at approximately the same time each day. This will help your milk production to be lower at that time and it will give other members of your family a chance to feed the baby.

If you wish, a daily routine bottle may be introduced at around 5:00 p.m., when you may feel most run down. In the event of extreme stress or exhaustion, your milk production may diminish and both you and your baby will benefit from a planned bottle. Keep in mind that the baby may not accept a bottle from you because he prefers breast milk, so it's helpful to have someone else available to provide the bottle. Or, you might replace the 2:00 a.m. feeding so that the baby's father can participate at that time and give you the additional sleep you so desperately need during this period.

Even though introducing a bottle at the same time each day will ultimately cause the breast to reduce milk production at that particular time, milk production will be just as good at the other feedings of the day. This is because of the stimulus of the baby's suckling and the production of milk which responds to it.

Returning to work

If you are planning to return to work, you may continue to breast-feed or you may wish to introduce a bottle. While you are away from the baby, you will need to replace the daytime feedings one by one with feedings of formula or expressed milk. Gradually, over the course of a four-week period, you can cut back on your milk production during the hours that you will be at work. When you are at work, the baby can have a bottle and when you're at home, she can breastfeed. What you do on the weekends will depend on your body's reaction to this routine. You may be able to breastfeed all day Saturday and Sunday and produce adequate milk without experiencing any problems on Monday when you return to work. Or you may have a very low milk supply and find yourself with a very hungry baby on the weekend. It's possible that on Monday, after the daytime stimulation of breastfeeding on Saturday and Sunday, your breasts may feel engorged and may even leak. It's just a matter of experimenting to decide the best strategy for meeting your particular needs. The best advice is to test out each situation and decide what works best for you.

You may want to continue to breastfeed exclusively even when you are back at work. This means pumping milk at the usual time of feeding in order to continue the normal routine. You can use a manual breast pump, an electric breast pump, or hand manipulation. Store the milk in a refrigerator at work. Label it carefully! The milk should be used within the next 24 hours or frozen. If you find it difficult to pump milk from the breast by hand, an electric breast pump can be a very effective way of extracting milk quickly. Electric pumps are expensive to buy, but you can rent one from a hospital or from a company that specializes in renting out medical equipment. Pumping allows your baby to get the benefits of breast milk during the first six to twelve months, even when you have returned to your former routine.

When to wean the baby from breastfeeding

The decision to wean the baby from breastfeeding is a highly personal one. It may also be culturally determined. In some areas breastfeeding for longer than a year is encouraged because of the poor food supply. In highly developed countries, where extreme poverty is not a problem, the issues are different. The benefits of breast milk are most important during the first four to six months of life. After babies have begun to consume a wide range of foods, the nutritional benefits of breast milk no longer make a major contribution to growth, development, or nutritional status. This, of course, assumes that the baby has no medical problems and is eating a full range of foods.

Bottle Feeding

One of the main concerns with feeding your baby formula is the preparation of the formula and maintaining the highest possible level of sanitation. Different types of formula have different methods of preparation and different shelf lives. Read each label carefully. Certain formulas are ready to serve and require no added water. They are easy to use but often expensive. Liquid concentrates require you to add water; if you give your baby the undiluted form, it could damage the baby's immature kidneys. Powdered formula is often the cheapest, but it should not be used for longer than four weeks after it has been opened. For a casual user of formula, this is wasteful. The type you choose will depend on your budget and on the frequency with which you plan to use formula.

You may find it convenient to prepare only one bottle at a time. Sterilize all the measuring and feeding instruments carefully before use. Wash your hands too. Add sterilized water to the liquid or powder (depending on the formula) and warm it for your baby. Don't use a microwave oven to warm the baby's bottle, because it will heat the liquid unevenly, leaving hot spots in the milk that can cause burns. You can keep formula bottles for one day in the refrigerator before you use them, but an unfinished bottle should be discarded immediately. If your baby has an allergic reaction to formula, try a soya formula. Talk to your pediatrician about any allergic reactions.

Don't try to make your own formula to save money. Homemade formulas do not provide the correct balance of nutrients that babies need. If you're considering bottle feeding, you must be prepared to accept the expense and responsibility of selecting the proper formula.

The timing of bottle feeding is different from that of breast-feeding. You cannot let your baby drink from one large bottle in fits and starts throughout the day, although this technique resembles the "on demand" schedule of the young breastfed baby. A schedule of small (2 to 3 oz or 50 to 75 mL) bottle feedings in the first few weeks will help establish a rhythm. During each feeding, pay careful attention to regular burping.

When babies are bottle fed, it is easy to see how much they have consumed. You may overfeed your baby if you encourage her to finish the bottle. Try to be fully attuned to your baby's appetite. This includes recognizing when she is hungry and when she is full and responding appropriately. While feeding on a schedule is easier to do with a bottle, feeding on demand is more natural and will allow the baby to regulate her own appetite.

Fussing and Feeding

It is not unusual for babies to fuss or cry between feedings. They may be quite happy to have something in the mouth even when they aren't hungry. Don't use water as a substitute for a pacifier or milk. A small infant drinking more than 8 oz (225 mL) of water at a feeding is at risk of water intoxication. Pacifiers are important to some infants because their need to suckle often exceeds their need for food. Without a pacifier, they may cry excessively for oral gratification. The pacifier will provide this without overfeeding the baby. Without a pacifier, most will eventually find a thumb or finger to suck. When the time comes, it is easier to wean them from the pacifier than from a thumb.

Over the course of the first few weeks, you may discover that your child has a specific time of day when she is especially fussy. After the first few months, your baby will develop a more regular routine of feeding and napping. Until this happens, however, there may be a fair bit of confusion. The duration of periods of crying and fussing seems to increase up until about six weeks and then decreases. Many infants cry during the evening hours and often into the late evening. Others may be fussiest from 4:00 a.m. to 7:00 a.m. or from 9:00 a.m. to 11:00 a.m. If your baby cries continuously and pulls up her legs with large volumes of gas, she has colic. If you are breastfeeding, your doctor might consider a change in your own diet. For formula-fed babies, a change in formula may be helpful. Babies differ widely when it comes to crying and fussing behaviours. Some families find the first few months very exciting (with the possible exception of those middle-of-the-night feedings!). For other families, those months are sheer torture, as the baby cries constantly. Endless days turn into sleepless nights and the stress level rises dangerously. Although this time seems like an eternity, either of these patterns will pass as the baby matures beyond the first several months. What each family needs is patience, perseverance, and some perspective. Just remind yourself that one day this child will actually take off with friends and ignore you!

Giving Vitamin and Mineral Supplements to Babies

The Canadian Paediatric Nutrition Committee has indicated that babies do not need nutrient supplementation from six to twelve months if they are getting formula fortified with iron and eating other foods which contain iron and vitamin C. The only supplement that may be recommended is vitamin D for the breastfed infant who gets little exposure to sunlight. Breastfed babies whose mothers are strict vegetarians will also need vitamins D and B_{12}. And fluoride supplements are recommended for breastfed babies who do not get fluoridated water. In spite of these recommendations, surveys show that 50 percent of babies get supplements. Supplements are unnecessary, except for infants who are at risk. These include babies who have erratic or poor food intake, infants who drink cow's milk instead of formula during the first year, and infants who are given unconventional diets, such as a strict vegetarian diet.

Most infants are given a vitamin K injection or drops immediately after birth because they are born without their own supply. Vitamin K helps to clot blood. In adults, vitamin K is produced by intestinal bacteria. A good dietary source is green leafy vegetables, but we don't rely on these when the bacteria are doing their job. Newborns have been in a sterile environment, however, and have no bacteria in their intestines at first. In order to make sure that they do not develop a bleeding problem after delivery (hemorrhagic disease of the newborn), hospitals give them vitamin K right after birth. After the first few days, they no longer need an injection unless they are placed on antibiotics, which wipe out those helpful bacteria.

Babies also need iron in their diets. A low level of iron in young children can cause learning and behaviour problems. This awareness of the importance of iron is reflected in recent changes in feeding recommendations for babies which promote the use of iron-fortified formulas for formula-fed babies for the first year of life. Babies who receive breast milk get iron in a form which is quickly absorbed, so they do not need iron supplements.

Introducing Solids

The decision to introduce solids is not always a simple one. At one time it was fashionable to give babies cereal as early as possible. Parents were rather competitive about their baby's diets and often boasted about the wide range of foods their babies would eat at a very early age. Nowadays we recognize that introducing foods too early is unwise. Babies cannot digest cereals until they are at least three months old. They will swallow them, but they get no nutrients from them. Eating cereals at too early an age may also mean that the baby is drinking less breast milk or formula. The early introduction to certain foods may set the stage for allergic reactions later on.

How can you tell when your baby is ready for solids? In general, the best indicators come from the infant. One sign babies give is that they are no longer satisfied with breast milk or formula alone. They might show this by continuing to cry for more after the bottle or breast is empty, or by waking up hungry in the middle of the night to eat after weeks of sleeping through the night. Another sign might be a slowing down of growth. You will find this out at the baby's routine health checkups when his weight and length are measured. This slowing down would suggest he needs extra calories from solid foods. A baby demonstrating interest in food eaten by other family members can sometimes also be an indication. Remember, however, that for the first four to six months, breast milk or formula can provide the baby with the most complete and nutritious food. In fact, this is the only time in our lives when a single food will do the job. After the signs of readiness for solids are confirmed, a new set of feeding practices needs to be introduced.

Dramatic changes take place from the sixth to the twelfth month of life. Babies go from a state of complete reliance on one food provided by others to feeding themselves a diet similar to that of the rest of the family. Throughout this period, keep feeding your baby either breast milk or iron-fortified formula. She should continue to receive as much breast milk, or formula as she wants along with her solids. Since mothers cannot tell how much breast milk their babies are getting, breastfed babies can continue to control their own intake. Gradually introduce food from all four food groups until the baby is eating a variety of healthy foods at the end of twelve months.

Do not give your baby regular milk before he is one year old— because it does not contain iron, it can irritate the stomach. However, if cow's milk must be used, make sure it is whole milk and not 2 percent or skim milk. This recommendation holds until your baby is two years old; it will ensure that he gets enough fat and not too many salts. Some parents take nutritional advice intended for adults and apply it to their babies. They do not realize the importance of fat in a baby's diet. Fat is needed for a baby's growth and development, especially for brain cells and nervous tissue.

The Canadian Paediatric Nutrition Committee recommends that the first weaning food for infants be iron-fortified cereal. This gives babies a good source of iron to coincide with the increased need for iron which occurs at four to six months of age. Introduce new foods one at a time and repeat them the next day, with a minimum three-day wait before you try an additional new item. This method will help to determine whether the baby has any allergic reaction to a particular food. Foods that are most likely to cause allergies, such as strawberries, peanuts, or seafood, should be introduced after one year. If there is a family history of allergy to particular foods, then those foods should be introduced much later.

The first time you give your baby cereal, she may have trouble getting it into her mouth. Prepare for a messy encounter and enjoy the ride. You can thin out the cereal with liberal amounts of breast milk or formula to make it easier for her to swallow. Once she can get the food from the spoon into her mouth, add less fluid to make a thicker mixture. Later, the cereal can be lumpy and you can add fruits for a more interesting flavour and texture. Gradually she will get used to the changing textures and learn how to handle these in her mouth. It takes time to develop chewing and swallowing skills. Patience and a positive attitude will go a long way in helping you and your baby to enjoy this new experience.

Start by giving your baby one to two tablespoons (15 to 25 mL) of cereal twice a day. Once he accepts the cereal, you can increase the volume of the feedings and time them to coincide with family meals. For example, within a month of getting him started on cereal, you can feed your baby 6 tablespoons (100 mL) of cereal with 3 oz (75 mL) of milk, either breast milk or formula, at approximately 7:00 a.m., 11:00 a.m., 4:00 p.m., or 7:00 p.m. Over time, you can adjust each of these "meals" to resemble breakfast, lunch, snack, and dinner. As you add new foods, the feedings will reflect the family's usual meal choices. Between meals, feed him breast milk or formula. As the meals become larger and more varied, your baby will need less and less milk between meals and snacks. After about twelve months he may eat only the meals and snacks, with milk as a starter for the day and at bedtime.

The recipe section for this chapter has a full range of food preparation instructions, including full dinners for baby.

Pay attention to the timing of meals and the amount of food you provide. When you introduce new foods, the baby should have a good appetite for them. It helps when she isn't too hungry or too full. Try feeding her milk from one breast or giving her the first half of a bottle, then introduce the new food, followed by breastfeeding from the other breast or from the remainder of the bottle. An alternative is to start with solids as between-breastfeeding "snacks."

Put a small amount of the baby's food on the end of the spoon and put the spoon towards the back of the baby's mouth. This will counter the extrusion reflex, which makes a baby spit out food with his tongue. This is not necessary with an older baby, who will quickly learn to move the food back himself. Never put cereal or mashed food in a bottle, because this may cause choking.

After cereal has been mastered, fruits or vegetables can be added gradually. They provide vitamin C as well as other important vitamins and minerals. Orange or dark green vegetables such as cooked carrots, peas, winter squash, or other foods high in beta-carotene may cause hypercarotenemia, a high blood level of carotene which may temporarily turn the baby's skin orange. This is quite harmless and disappears when the foods are reduced. Other foods to avoid during the weaning period are home-prepared spinach, turnips, carrot soup, and carrot juice, which can cause another blood problem (met-hemoglobinemia). This is because of the nitrite in these products. The nitrite levels rise when these foods are stored in the refrigerator for one or more days. For variety, use green beans, well-cooked cauliflower, and summer squashes (which are not as high in beta-carotene).

Some fruits and vegetables can be eaten raw. Banana, papaya, and avocado are ideal because of their mushy texture. Don't be alarmed by the brown fibres they leave behind in your baby's diaper.

The last food group to be added is the meat group; this includes meat, eggs, fish, and cheese. Canned fish, mashed without the bones, is a good source of protein. Other protein-rich foods include yogurt, peas, well-cooked beans, and lentils, which provide protein sources similar to meat products. In the meantime, add pasta, rice, mashed potatoes, breads, and other starchy foods to form a more complete meal.

You may find it relaxing to prepare and feed the baby his food before the family meal when you have the extra time and attention needed for the job. Make sure everything you use is clean.

At six to nine months of age, your baby can accept naturally soft foods, which can be mashed and introduced without a great deal of preparation. These include banana, avocado, papaya, applesauce, and well-cooked vegetables. Cooked meat, fruits, and vegetables should be crushed through a sieve to make them the right texture for young babies to swallow and digest. Food processors or baby food grinders are ideal at this time. In addition, you can use commercially prepared infant foods which are manufactured in factories under the highest possible standards of cleanliness. These foods are convenient and well tolerated by infants. However, they may be somewhat expensive. Check the prices for yourself.

Foods for your baby can be frozen in small meal-sized batches and reheated as needed. If you reheat them in the microwave, be sure to stir them carefully to distribute the heat. Remember that the microwave oven can create hot spots in food that can burn your baby's mouth.

The weaning diet should be based on a diet of breast milk or formula with the gradual addition of foods that are typical of your family's food. Eventually, all four food groups will give the baby the nutrients and energy necessary to meet her requirements for growth and development.

Finger Foods and Self-feeding

As soon as your baby can transfer an object from her hand to her mouth, you can give her hard rolls or biscuits to support the skill required for self-feeding. This skill often appears when a baby is teething. A hard bagel or teething biscuit can provide some comfort to her gums. Do not use foods that break up easily in the mouth and can cause choking.

From eight to twelve months, babies develop the pincer reflex, which allows them to pick up small food pieces between thumb and forefinger. Some people call this the "Cheerio stage" because you can prepare small pieces of cereal, meat, fruit, and vegetable and the baby can feed himself at last. During this time you can add an increasing variety of food to his diet, such as pieces of toast or grilled cheese sandwiches.

During the first year, do not give your child honey and corn syrup, because they have been known to contain the spores of the organism that causes botulism. Children under three should not be given foods that could cause choking or aspiration, such as whole nuts, large peas or beans, popcorn, grapes, or large berries. Other foods to avoid are hot dogs cut up into slices that would block the throat, or foods that form balls in the mouth, such as peanut butter sandwiches. Keep sweets to a minimum because they cause tooth decay and because they take up space that should be used for more nutritious foods. As soon as your baby's teeth erupt, they are vulnerable to dental decay. Brush or wipe your baby's teeth clean with a cloth or soft toothbrush after meals and before bed. And never put a baby to bed with a bottle. The sugar in the fruit juice, milk, or sweetened drink will cause cavities if the liquid stays in the baby's mouth overnight. Two ways of avoiding this problem are to encourage the use of a drinking cup as soon as your baby can manage one and to clean his teeth before bedtime.

By twelve to eighteen months of age, your baby can consume most of the food that the other members of your family eat. Your main goal at this time is to encourage her to enjoy a variety of foods and to develop some independence in feeding. With patience, persuasion, and perseverance you'll enjoy the stages of feeding your child successfully.

How Much Food Do Babies Need?

Some babies are far more active than others and need more food; others are passive or slow growers and need fewer calories. These differences are based on a combination of genetic predisposition and individual characteristics. The general health of a baby will also affect her appetite. When a baby is ill, her appetite may decrease. This is often the first sign of a cold or flu. When she feels better, her appetite returns and her growth catches up. Feed your child to meet her particular appetite. Do not force feed her, but try to ensure that she gets enough calories to keep her healthy. Of course, this can be easier said than done. I've encouraged my children to take just one more bite only to have them throw up on the plate after eating beyond their appetite. You really shouldn't mess with Mother Nature.

The Second Year

During a child's second year, the rapid growth that was typical of the first year begins to slow down. You may notice that your child is less hungry and less interested in food. It is important to recognize that it is growth which drives appetite, not the other way around. Forcing babies to eat will not make them grow any faster, but may teach them to hate food, or to overeat.

You may, however, find that your child has become more curious about food and may seek out food by sampling things around the house. Desires for pet food, ice, or other strange requests may be signs of an iron deficiency.

During this time, children enjoy finger foods which are easily handled, such as cut-up fruits and vegetables, crackers, cheese slices, and dry pieces of cereal. Give your child small amounts at a time to minimize the mess. Your child may insist on feeding herself and should not be rushed. If this causes problems with the rest of the family, start her mealtime early, so that she gets a head start. Allow her all the time she needs to eat in peace. If she is eating cereal, give her a glass of milk to go along with it to make the most of the cereal's nutritional value. This is an important time when children develop skills and new pride in their abilities to feed themselves.

Snacks

It is important to plan snacks so that they contribute good nutrition to the overall diet. Snacks can include cheese and crackers, vegetables and dip, cut-up fruits, or cereal. Avoid foods that cause choking and don't let your toddler walk, play, or run around with food in his mouth. As children get older, they may be tempted to play games by catching tossed food in their mouths. This can also lead to choking.

During the second year, your child needs whole milk, not skim milk. However, 2 percent milk may be advisable in certain cases such as obesity. Discuss this concern with the baby's doctor. Eggs and previously avoided foods such as seafood can be introduced at this time. Some children want specific foods such as eggs or peanut butter sandwiches every day. My first son liked tuna sandwiches so much that he had them for breakfast! Now, he won't even take them to school for lunch. It is not unusual for children to go on food jags. Don't worry about this unless it lasts for many months.

The most disconcerting part about feeding the child between ages one and two comes when their growth starts to slow down and their appetite plummets. This is normal. As long as you provide healthy foods you know they enjoy, your child will eat well and thrive.

RECIPES

INTRODUCING SOLIDS TO YOUR BABY IS AN EXCITING NEW STAGE. Follow the order recommended by your baby's doctor and you will be surprised by the fun you'll have trying new foods. When I was making Mira's baby food, I used very simple guidelines. Following Rena's expert advice, I found the process to be not only challenging, but indeed great fun! I hope you will agree.

First Vegetables

Carrots

Scrub and peel 2 bunches fresh carrots, slice on diagonal.

To make in microwave, place carrots in pyrex dish, add 3 to 4 tbsp (50 to 75 mL) water, cover, and cook on High for 5 to 6 minutes. Check to make sure they are very tender. To make in steamer, cover and steam over boiling water 7 to 10 minutes.

Put carrots in blender or processor. Purée until consistency is a soft mush. Add a little boiling water until the consistency that you want has been achieved. Spoon into ice cube trays. Cover and freeze. Put cubes into plastic bags, remove air. Date and label the bags and return to freezer. When serving the carrots, remove one frozen cube at a time. Leave at room temperature to defrost, then place in a baby food warming dish until warm enough to serve.

When first introducing vegetables, make sure that they are very soft and mushy. As the baby gets older, more texture can be added. If you are using the microwave, be very careful to defrost evenly. Test the food to make sure that it is evenly warmed.

Frozen Peas

Place $2\frac{1}{2}$ cups (625 mL) frozen peas in 4 tbsp (60 mL) water in microwave, covered, and cook on High for 4 minutes. Purée in blender or food processor until desired consistency. Freeze and label as recommended for carrots. To steam: place peas in steamer, cover, and simmer over boiling water 6 to 8 minutes until tender. Makes one ice cube tray.

Sweet Potatoes and Yams

Peel and cut 3 medium sweet potatoes or yams into 1 x 2-inch (2 x 5 cm) cubes. Microwave, covered, on High 7 to 8 minutes until tender and soft. Purée according to instructions for carrots or steam over boiling water 12 to 15 minutes until tender. Purée and freeze as usual. Makes one ice cube tray.

Winter Squashes

Acorn, squash, butternut, hubbard—all are sweet and delicious. Scrub outside and cut 1 butternut or hubbard squash or 2 acorn squash into large chunks. Microwave, covered, on High for 5 minutes. Turn around and microwave additional 4 to 5 minutes until squash is soft. Scrape squash from skin. Purée in blender or processor with a little water until desired consistency. Or steam covered over 2 inches (5 cm) boiling water 18 to 20 minutes until soft. Spoon into ice cube trays and freeze according to instructions for carrots. Makes two ice cube trays.

First Fruits

Applesauce

Wash, peel, core, and seed 6 to 8 apples. Cut into large chunks. Place in bowl, cover. Place in microwave 2 to 3 minutes until soft. Purée in blender until soft. Fill ice cube trays and freeze. Remove from trays. Place in plastic freezer bags, remove air, date, and label.

Bananas

Mash ¼ ripe banana very well with a fork. Add ½ tsp (2 mL) formula. Make sure that the banana is very soft and mashed completely. Give small portions to the baby.

Avocados

Mash ¼ ripe avocado very well with a fork. Ripe avocados should mash very easily with a fork. Overripe avocados have an unpleasant taste which your baby will not like.

Papayas

Mash ⅛ ripe papaya very well with a fork.

Mangoes

Mash a few tablespoons and serve to baby.

Peaches

Peel and slice 3 to 4 peaches or nectarines. Place in bowl and cover. Microwave 1 to 2 minutes until very soft. Purée in blender or processor and freeze. Peaches should be cooked initially. A few months later they can be introduced raw.

Foods for Babies Eight Months or Older

Vegetables

Wash and peel 4 to 5 small white turnips or 1 yellow turnip. Cut into small chunks. Steam for 4 to 6 minutes in a microwave in small amount of water until soft. Purée in blender or processor with 1 tbsp (15 mL) apple juice. Spoon into ice cube trays, cover, and freeze. Transfer to bag, remove air, label, and date.

Other vegetables suitable for eight-month-old babies include broccoli, asparagus, and zucchini. Prepare using same method as for turnips.

Last Introduction of Vegetables

Use 12 oz (340 g) package frozen white baby corn kernels. Place in bowl and cover. Microwave 6 to 7 minutes on High until very soft. Purée in blender with a little water or formula. Freeze in ice cube trays, covered. Place in bags, remove air, date, and label.

Introduce beets, brussels sprouts, peeled and seeded raw cucumber.

Fruits

Cantaloupe, honeydew melon, grapes (peeled and mashed).

Introducing Meats

Mama Rozzie's Chicken Soup
Purée some meat from chicken with broth to a smooth consistency. Pour into ice cube trays, cover, and freeze. Transfer cubes to freezer bag. Remove air and label, date, and freeze. This should be the first meat introduced to your baby.

Dinners for Baby

New foods should be introduced one at a time. Once the baby has been fed a new food over the course of three to four days and had no adverse reaction, the new food can be blended with others to make complete dinners.

General Directions for Complete Baby Dinners

1. Simmer together all of the ingredients in a saucepan on medium heat for 20 minutes.

2. Pour all of the mixture into a food processor, blend, and serve.

3. Leftovers will not freeze well if they contain potato; other dinners will freeze well. Do not save foods that have been left over on the feeding dish.

4. Initially the mixture should be very smooth. Add more water if necessary to get a smoother texture. As baby gets older, less water and blending are necessary.

Veal Scallopini Dinner
3 oz (100 mg) veal
4 oz (125 mL) carrots, fresh or frozen
1 small potato, peeled and diced
4 oz (100 mL) water

Harvest Chicken Dinner
1 boneless chicken breast
½ cup (125 mL) cooked rice
½ cup (125 mL) winter squash, peeled and diced
½ cup (125 mL) water or chicken broth

Maritime Dinner
3 oz (75 g) boneless and skinless halibut or salmon
1 small boiled potato
¼ cup (50 mL) peas, fresh or frozen
⅓ cup (75 mL) water

Asian Chicken
1 small boneless chicken breast
½ cup (125 mL) rice noodles
½ cup (125 mL) peas
Dash low-sodium soy sauce (optional)
½ cup (125 mL) water or chicken broth

Spaghetti à l'enfant
½ cup (125 mL) cooked pasta, any shape
3 oz (75 g) ground veal cooked in ½ cup (125 mL) tomato sauce

CHILDHOOD

THE NEWEST NUTRITION RECOMMENDATIONS FOR Canadians are designed to reduce some of the chronic diseases known to be linked with diet. These include obesity, cardiovascular disease, and cancer. These recommendations are primarily intended for the adult population, even though they claim to be intended for anyone over the age of two. They include maintaining a healthy weight; reducing total dietary fat; increasing complex carbohydrates (starch and fibre); and limiting sugar, salt, caffeine, and alcohol. However, there are no guarantees that following the perfect diet (even if such a thing exists) will prevent you or your children from getting a chronic disease.

The application of these recommendations to young children should be accompanied by an understanding of their unique needs. Overzealous calorie and fat restriction can interfere with children's growth and development. The information in this chapter should help parents to understand their children's nutritional needs.

The practical application of the nutrition recommendations for Canadians is *Canada's Food Guide to Healthy Eating*, launched in 1992. In the second half of this section, we will show you how to apply *Canada's Food Guide to Healthy Eating* to planning your children's menus. There are simple, reliable, kid-tested recipes that combine good nutrition with good eating. Note that the recipes are not intended for children with special dietary problems such as allergies, lactose intolerance, diabetes, and so forth. Consultation with a dietitian as well as a local organization dedicated to each of these problems is recommended.

Choosing Healthy Diets

Your goal as a parent, when it comes to feeding your children, is to ensure that they grow to be strong and healthy. You can help them develop a positive attitude towards eating a variety of interesting and nutritious foods. Start by accepting that they have a certain body shape, which may not be the average shape. Some parents fret over their child's height (too short, too tall) and others over their weight (too thin, too fat). Much of the worry is rooted in their own experiences of childhood, particularly if they themselves were ridiculed because of their size or shape. These parents may become overanxious about their children's eating habits, hoping somehow to influence their growth and development.

We hope the information in this section will help parents overcome these concerns and enable them to form more positive attitudes towards food and eating. They'll not only help their children, but themselves as well.

Many parents believe that childhood eating habits will persist throughout adulthood. Some are terrified by the prospect that their children will eat nothing but chicken fingers and peanut butter sandwiches for the next eighty years. But think back to what you ate as a child. Now think about the foods you have learned to enjoy since then. Most adults learn to appreciate a wider variety of foods as they grow up and chances are that your kids will want a more interesting menu one day.

Another myth about children and food that has been around for many years is that children have an inborn ability to select a balanced diet. In the 1920s, a researcher by the name of Dr. Clara Davis studied very young children and their ability to select a nutritious diet. She provided them with a wide range of healthy foods and demonstrated that they did, in fact, choose foods from all four food groups. However, only the most nutritious foods were available. The children were offered fruits, vegetables, meats, cereals, and milk. There were no cakes, candies, or soda pop to choose from. Their willingness to select a good diet from the foods available was really a test of their curiosity and not their nutritional wisdom. However, the experiment did show that children naturally prefer variety in their diets as opposed to monotony. Unfortunately, this research was misinterpreted by others who believed that children would choose a healthy diet if left to their own devices. This is only true when children are offered exclusively healthy choices and no so-called junk food.

In our society we have a wide range of food choices, including cookies, chips, candy, and pop, just to mention a few examples. Try to think of these foods as "sometimes foods." They will not do your child any harm when they are part of an otherwise well-balanced diet. But they do take up space that could be used for more nutritious foods. And for some children there may be a limit to the space they are willing to fill. Think of the foods that are high in vitamins, minerals, and other nutrients as "everyday food." These are the ones that make up the four food groups. You may need to do a little promotion on these foods to compete with the heavily advertised "sometimes foods." These labels might help to remove the notion of "good" and "bad" foods. The biggest danger in using the "good food" and "bad food" labels is that we begin to label ourselves when we eat them. How often have you said, "I was bad today," when you are talking about eating so-called "bad foods"? How often have people told you that they have been "good," when they were really talking about what they ate? Must we measure our personal worth by the foods we eat? Are we setting the stage for eating disorders in our children when we impose this sort of baggage on them?

There are no such things as bad foods, only bad diets. Take, for example, a chocolate bar, which is high in sugar and fat and low in nutrients. As part of a diet made up of a balance of the food groups, the chocolate bar can add energy to the total daily intake. However, if you eat that chocolate bar with a can of soda pop as lunch after a morning without breakfast, then it represents a major portion of the day's intake and is a poor food choice. It is the context in which we choose a single food which is important, not the food itself.

In order to ensure that your children consume a wide variety of highly nutritious foods, it's up to you to set good examples through your own eating habits. Nothing is more damaging to parents' credibility than to insist that their children eat fruits and vegetables while they eat chips and candy. I have also seen parents tell their children that they cannot have dessert and then sit down to their own heaping serving of pie or cake. Parents can be most helpful to their children when they try to establish a positive attitude towards trying new foods, consume a healthy diet, and keep food in perspective. Be prepared to practise what you preach.

You can ensure that your children get all the nutrients they need from food (rather than from supplements) as long as you provide them with servings from each of the four food groups.

Most of us learned about these groups in our early school years and have used them as a mental checklist from time to time ever since. The newest Canadian food guide, released in 1992, recommends that children have two servings of meat or meat alternative products each day. *Canada's Food Guide to Healthy Eating* was designed for children over four with the following recommendations. We have added our own suggestions for children under four.

Recommended Serving Sizes		
	4 and older	**under 4**
Meat & Alternates	2–4 oz meat,	2 oz
2–3 servings/day	⅓ cup beans, tofu	2 tbsp
	2 tbsp peanut butter	1 tbsp
Milk	1 cup milk	½ cup milk
2–3 servings/day	2 oz cheese	1 oz cheese
Fruits and Vegetables	1 fruit	½ fruit
5–10 servings	½ cup vegetables	¼ cup vegetables
Breads & Cereals	1 oz cereal	½ oz cereal
5–12 servings	½ cup pasta or rice	¼ cup pasta or rice
	1 slice bread	½ slice bread

These are recommended serving sizes and are not meant to be a rigid prescription. The number of servings and amounts will vary for each child according to his appetite. Remember that health, growth and activity all influence appetite from day to day. In addition to these food groups, you can add various oils and fats and sweeteners to round out the overall diet.

These guidelines consider foods as the raw materials for meals and recipes. Naturally, families from different heritages will combine them in very different ways to create unique meals. They are still an excellent tool for parents and others responsible for children's diets to use when assessing whether there are any foods missing from the child's diet on a day-to-day basis. You can use them not only in meal and snack planning but also for shopping or selecting from a restaurant menu.

Unfortunately, there can be a downside to pushing your children to eat a good diet. When you become overly concerned about whether your children are eating the more nutritious foods, such as meats or vegetables, you often send them mixed messages. Typically parents bribe children to eat healthy foods by rewarding them with less healthy choices. For example, we tell children that turnips are good for them and if they eat them, they will be rewarded with ice cream. Children quickly figure out that if they have to be rewarded for eating their vegetables, then vegetables must not taste very good. Similarly, they realize that a food used for reward tastes good and is probably bad for them. As a result, children start to assume that healthy foods taste bad and that good-tasting foods are unhealthy. An alternative is to make the majority of the offerings healthy and allow the child some choice.

Remember, your children may not share your taste in food, for a number of reasons. Children are more sensitive than adults to food temperature. If a child burns her mouth on a specific food such as soup or pizza, she may retain a negative association with that food that goes beyond her exact memory of the event. As a result she will avoid that food for a long time before trying it again. Also, children have more taste buds than adults and therefore are more sensitive to stronger flavours in foods. This explains why some children have a natural dislike for certain foods with strong flavours, such as vegetables or meats. As a general rule, they prefer sweet and mild flavours. Children are also more resistant to certain textures than adults. Most of them dislike the slimy texture of foods such as cooked asparagus, spinach, or mushrooms, and prefer crisp and crunchy foods such as crackers or raw carrots. Eventually, most children come to accept a wider variety of foods as a result of changes in perception or as a result of the repeated introduction of these foods. Some researchers have found that in order for a child to become familiar with a food or even to be willing to try a food, you may have to present it as many as ten to fifteen times!

Obviously it requires enormous patience and persistence to get children to eat certain vegetables, and, frankly, it may not be necessary. Instead of fighting over spinach as a source of folic acid and beta-carotene, offer them orange juice or carrots. Orange juice is loaded with folic acid and vitamin C, and a few carrot sticks provide plenty of beta-carotene. Keep in mind that the food group includes both fruits and vegetables. There is no harm in focusing on the fruits while giving children the small number of vegetables they actually like to eat. Remember what you ate as a child. Over the course of time, you came to enjoy broccoli, eggplant, and mushrooms. Instead of fighting over vegetables, consider other strategies to ensure that your children get a complete diet. Keep in mind their natural preferences for mild, sweet, crispy, and crunchy foods. Put raw vegetables in a salad or serve them with their favourite dressing as a dip. Hide them in soups and sandwiches. Disguise meats in spaghetti sauce or in hero sandwiches. Ask your children to help you plan the family's menus. Then sit back and pray for success.

Meal Patterns

Parents who hope to stay sane while coping with work, child care, and other responsibilities want to avoid the "restaurant syndrome" at mealtimes. That's what happens when each person in the family chooses different foods for dinner. The alternative is making one family meal for all adults and children of different ages. This could unfortunately translate into meals which represent the lowest common denominator. In other words, to avoid conflict, the parents end up eating only those foods the children are willing to eat. This gets very boring and turns mealtimes into chores instead of pleasant experiences. There is a huge personal incentive for parents to encourage children to eat a wide range of interesting recipes.

Children are influenced, not only by their parents, but by other children. You can take advantage of this situation to expand your child's eating habits. Often a child will try a new food in the presence of a friend or when he is away from home. This is one of those times we are happy to see children succumb to peer pressure. It is always worthwhile to ask children when they return from summer camp, day care, or a school trip whether they discovered any new foods. If the answer is yes, it may be possible to add something new to the family eating pattern. One summer, my kids came home from camp asking for tacos and submarine sandwiches. Of course, no system is completely foolproof. I'll never forget the boy who begged his mother for Spam after enjoying it on a canoe trip only to spit it out when she finally served it! Some foods lose their meaning when eaten out of context.

Another opportunity to outsmart the opposition is to introduce new foods to children when they have friends visiting. Your chances are even better when you have a known "good eater" as a guest. In the presence of their friends, your children may try new foods that they wouldn't touch with only the family around the table.

Even after children have become accustomed to a varied and healthy diet, it pays to sustain their interest with appropriate meal routines. Children need both physical and emotional comfort at mealtimes to ensure a healthy appetite. Seat very small children at a low table or on a booster seat with utensils that are small enough for them to use independently. Make sure that they have plenty of time and no deadlines to meet. The amount of food on the plate should match their capacity to eat it, so that they are not over-whelmed by the task. A room that is free of distractions such as toys, television, and other activities will allow them to concentrate on the food. Even a table piled with magazines and books will provide sufficient distraction to keep them from eating. When the radio plays their favourite song, don't be surprised if they leave the table to imitate the latest rock video. Above all, let them respond to their own appetite and don't force them to clean their plates.

Emotional comfort is just as important at mealtime as physical comfort and desirable food. Meals can be a time for friendly family discussions or fierce confrontation. The cues will generally come from the adults in charge. It's hard to eat when people are discussing upsetting or revolting subjects. The mention of a dirty diaper or worms in food can bring an abrupt stop to an otherwise pleasant experience. Sibling bickering can have the same effect. Set the mood for eating just as you set the table.

Although many North American families have settled into a pattern of a small breakfast, small lunch, and large dinner, this pattern does not work for everyone. One child may be able to eat a large breakfast and lunch but arrive for dinner with a very small appetite. Others are not hungry at all in the morning but can eat well by the evening.

Research suggests that it is best to eat most of our calories in the earlier part of the day. In any case, know the natural appetite pattern for each child and work with it rather than against it. If your child's appetite peaks do not coincide with the usual pattern, plan meals to provide samples from all food groups when she is hungry. Serve full-course meals for breakfast or lunch with lighter fare for dinner, if that will ensure a good day's nutrition.

Breakfast

Children and teenagers may want to skip breakfast. Studies show they are unlikely to make up the missed nutrients during the rest of the day. In general about 25 percent of the day's total energy should come from breakfast. Because of the foods we most often include, breakfast provides us with an important set of nutrients. That is because we generally include a fruit, giving us a stable source of vitamin C, grains (such as rice and bread) or cereals (hot or cold) providing healthy carbohydrates, and milk, which provides protein, calcium, and vitamin D. Your child may not get these foods at other meals. Without breakfast, a child could fall short of the daily needs for each of those nutrients.

The reason for skipping breakfast may be related to the breakfast habits of the parents (as many as 18 percent of adults have only coffee or tea for breakfast) or to the fact that both parents may be working and children are left to prepare their own breakfast. Given the choice of sleeping late, watching television, or preparing their own breakfast, most children will opt to skip breakfast. Another reason children skip breakfast is their personal concern about weight. All the evidence about weight maintenance indicates that eating breakfast is essential to keeping a healthy weight. Most of the calories that are missed when breakfast is skipped are made up during the rest of the day, but the nutrients are not. Skipping breakfast does not help anyone to lose weight.

When children skip breakfast, they often have more difficulty performing tasks at school. They may have trouble concentrating because blood glucose, the only source of energy for the brain, has run down since their last meal twelve to fifteen hours before. Without that source of energy, many experience nausea and fatigue and have consistently poor performance on standard achievement tests. Teachers can often identify the children who have not had breakfast because of their apathetic or irritable attitude during the morning. For this reason, many school districts have introduced breakfast programs to ensure that children who don't eat breakfast at home do get breakfast at school. These programs have been evaluated and they provide proof that breakfast can enhance children's behaviour and learning.

It is easy to get kids to eat cereal in the mornings. It does not much matter which cereal you pick. There are some on the market that are made of whole grains, but almost every breakfast cereal is fortified with a similar level of nutrients. If your children like the sweetened cereals and refuse the whole grain ones, don't argue. Just make sure they brush their teeth afterwards. It is not worth fighting with children to get them to eat breakfast when they are getting what they need from their favourite cereal. It's also helpful to remember that many outgrow their preference for the sweeter cereals or get bored with them eventually.

Protein at the breakfast meal helps keep energy levels high throughout the morning by helping sustain blood glucose levels for several hours. Eggs and milk are not the only sources of protein you can have for breakfast. Consider peanut butter, tuna, cheese, or other meat alternatives. Our granola recipe (page 57) and pancakes are also worth trying.

Snacks

Like mealtimes, snacks can become a source of conflict for children and parents. Unlike adults, very young children need snacks between meals to ensure that they get an adequate intake of the food groups. Until they are six, children will benefit from a mid-morning snack as well as an afternoon one. This routine has been built into many school kindergarten programs. Once children reach the first grade, there is no particular reason to provide most of them with snacks to eat during school hours. They should be using recess time for activity instead. Unfortunately, there has been so much promotion of children's snack foods that some school yards look like garbage dumps at the end of the recess period.

For kids who need a snack, after school is an ideal time. These snacks can provide a good opportunity to encourage young children to eat fruits and nutrient-dense foods (such as milk, cheese, and rolls) that they might not eat at meals. One way of ensuring this is to present children with a variety of attractive and healthy snacks after school and in the evening. If your cupboards are full of chips, candies, and other "sometimes foods," don't blame your children for eating them. Instead, plan and prepare snacks for children when they get home from school. These could include a fruit platter, vegetables and fresh yogurt dip, oatmeal cookies, and milk. We have some great snack recipes at the end of this section. Most children will not go to the trouble of taking fruit out of the refrigerator, washing it, and cutting it up, but they will gladly eat fruit if it is presented to them when they are hungry.

A planned snack time also prevents the problem of the

revolving kitchen door and the tracking of food all over the house. Even more important, the timing of snacks can also keep children from spoiling their appetite for meals. Provide snacks at least one and a half to two hours before meals so that your child's appetite can recover in time for dinner. In fact, some children find it easier to eat a well-balanced dinner when they are moderately hungry rather than "ravenous." Very young children cannot recognize that they are hungry and may express their hunger in cranky behaviour which can derail a well-planned meal.

School Lunches

Parents often complain about the monotony of preparing school lunches. It's not just the task that becomes monotonous, but the foods themselves. It is not unusual for children to request a peanut butter sandwich every single day!

Our suggestions have three purposes. First, all of us (especially kids) are concerned about the environment and schools are trying to encourage litter-free lunches. So we will focus on foods that can be packed with a minimum of waste. Second, the meals must be nutritious; *Canada's Food Guide to Healthy Eating* is, as always, a good tool for planning these meals. Third, children must like the food. This prevents waste and ensures that they don't trade away your masterpieces for something that is below your high standards.

Sandwiches are convenient to prepare, pack, and eat. Draw up a list of sandwiches each child is willing to eat so that when you find yourself in a rut, you can refer to this list. You can often get kids to eat vegetables by including them in sandwiches. Add lettuce and tomato to a turkey sandwich and you have a "sub." To make sure that you have a fresh (not a soggy) sub, pack the lettuce and tomato in a plastic container and let your child put the sandwich together at school. Other vegetables that make sandwiches more interesting are alfalfa sprouts and thinly sliced cucumbers. Use a separate container to keep it all fresh. If you add mayonnaise to sandwich fillings, spread the fillings on frozen bread to keep the sandwich cold longer. Another way to keep sandwiches cool is to freeze the drink you include. As the drink thaws during the morning, the food stays cold. Try some of the exciting party sandwiches at the end of the recipe section. They can be made ahead and frozen. Add fruit for dessert or fruit juice in your own container. Encourage your school to sell milk at lunch time for those who would like milk because this food will not keep well through the morning in a lunch bag.

One worthwhile investment is a thermal food jar. You can send soups, stews, or pasta dishes in them. This provides a great change from sandwiches and the food really stays warm. It works especially well if you fill the jar with hot water as you prepare the food. Dump the water, add the lunch, and you will be amazed at how warm the food stays during the day. In fact, even leftovers come home warm! Try sending our vegetable pea soup or macaroni and cheese as a main course. You can also send leftover pastas or quesadillas. Round out the meal with fruit, oatmeal cookies, and a drink.

Once children have access to their own money, they have new-found freedom to buy foods that you might not have in your house. A few basic principles are worth keeping in mind. First, children need to learn how to make purchasing decisions at some point. They need to learn that money can be saved for something special as well as spent impulsively on an attractive candy or toy. Buying chocolate bars or chips on their way to or from school can be an expensive routine and will wipe out their wallets (as long as you don't simply give them more money).

Second, the snacks they buy may simply add extra calories to their intake and may not ruin their appetite for meals. As long as they are growing well and brushing their teeth regularly, there is unlikely to be any problem. A worse problem is created when they are led to believe that these foods are somehow very special or very bad and they become secretive about eating them. Finally, children should feel secure knowing that all the food they really need is provided at home and that they do not have to use their own money to feed themselves.

Growth, Development, and Appetite

To find out whether your children are growing and gaining weight adequately, take them for regular medical checkups. You shouldn't need to weigh and measure your children at home. In fact, I think home weigh scales should be abolished! They create unnecessary anxiety and fear.

Normally, children will have growth spurts during specific

stages in their lives. The most common times are during the pre-school period between the ages of four and six and again during the pre-adolescent period between the ages of ten and thirteen. During these times it is common for children's appetite to increase. Remember that the stimulus for appetite comes from the growth itself and not the other way around. You cannot make a child grow more or faster by feeding him extra food.

Children should continue to eat to their own appetites as they did when they were infants. When children keep in touch with their appetites and with the signals from their bodies which tell them when they are hungry and when they are full, they will avoid the dangers brought on by an early preoccupation with weight. Children should never be forced to eat; nor should food be withheld from them when they are truly hungry. Food should be used to provide nourishment and not as an activity or as a reward. Otherwise children may learn to use foods to escape from boredom or to reward themselves for non-energy-spending activities. Although food offers us great pleasure and should be an enjoyable experience, the regular use of food as an escape from boredom or as a reward can set the stage for obesity or other eating disorders in later years.

It is possible to spoil children's appetites for good food. Giving a child a snack just before a meal will cause a change in appetite. Research has shown that high-carbohydrate food, such as fruit, bread, or crackers before meals will decrease total intake and may make children eat more protein. One might take advantage of this theory and try giving children a small carbohydrate snack before dinner to encourage their consumption of meat. On the other hand, eating a protein snack such as cheese, milk or sliced meats before a meal will make the child favour carbohydrates as the major calorie source during the meal.

In addition to foods that spoil the appetite, children may lose their appetite if they are overtired. Let the children have some quiet time after an active day at school; even if this means letting them flop in front of the television for half an hour before dinner. This is a good opportunity for them to unwind from the physical, mental, and social activities of the day and build up their appetite for dinner.

Other appetite spoilers are distractions, such as the desire to rush from the table to see a favourite television program. Activities planned for immediately after dinner such as sports, games, or special events can also put a damper on eating. Arguing or teasing each other at the table can also spoil appetites. Unfortunately, children often recover their appetites soon after the kitchen has been cleaned and may grab cookies, candies, or cakes to fill the void. The policy in our household is that "the kitchen is closed" after it has been cleaned. To protect parents from that revolving kitchen door with kids eating continuously between meals, the emphasis on good eating behaviour needs to be supported with appropriate time, place, and food selection to ensure that children get adequate nutrition at mealtimes.

Healthy Weights

Growth in height and weight is a normal part of childhood. Unfortunately, our society has become phobic about weight gain in adults and this has been transmitted to young children who have also become preoccupied with their weight. Girls may begin to worry about it as early as five or six years of age, and their concern may be related to the effect of television as much as to the influence of parents and other role models who are preoccupied with their own weight.

A survey in the United States of children between grades 3 and 6 demonstrated an extraordinary obsession with weight and thinness. Of the group of children studied, 45 percent said that they wanted to be thinner and 37 percent said they had already tried to lose weight. Six percent of the children under the age of 13 were eating so little that they were close to the condition of anorexia nervosa. A survey of adolescents revealed even higher proportions. Seventy percent of teenagers said that they were fat and 37 percent were dieting at the time of survey.

Children as young as five show a desire to avoid obesity and soon after the age of five begin to understand the relationship between eating and obesity. Children have been known to restrict their diets to the point at which they have actually stopped growing. If this happens, they may not achieve their normally expected height. In order to prevent this kind of behaviour, parents should have a healthy attitude about their own weight. Once they have achieved this, they will be able to impart to their children a healthy attitude towards growth and development. This is not an easy task when 70 percent of Canadian women indicated in a recent survey that they are trying to lose weight— even when they are well within the range of healthy weights.

Genetics plays an important role in determining body shape and composition. Whenever I am in a mall or a park where families are walking together, I am always impressed by the similarities in the size and shape of parents and their children. Part of the story is the way the family eats, but recently it has become clear that genetics is a major factor. Studies of identical twins raised apart show that they are more likely to resemble each other in weight than their adopted siblings. Surveys also show that if one parent is obese, then a child has a 50 percent chance of being obese. If both parents are obese, the chances for the child are 80 percent. Parents concerned about the genetic potential they pass on to their children need to first come to terms with their own weight and then develop a positive strategy to ensure that their children develop healthy eating and exercise patterns.

In addition to providing good nutrition, demonstrate your support for healthy physical activities. Your whole family can enjoy activities such as walking, biking, swimming, or sports together. Participation is important for the development of positive health behaviours and positive attitudes towards our bodies. All members of the family should be encouraged to participate in daily physical activities, especially ones that develop skills which can be carried on through adulthood. Sports such as tennis, skiing, or soccer are energy-demanding sports that are lots of fun for children and are easy to pursue through adult life. Noncompetitive forms of dance, figure skating, and swimming can also be healthy activities. Encouraging a good variety of physical activities enhances physical and skeletal development and coordination and encourages children to develop self-esteem and a positive self-image, as well as good sporting attitudes and control over their bodies and their emotions.

In addition to family involvement, we need to lobby for strong physical education programs in the schools. These should provide children not only fitness and fun but a sense of discipline and the knowledge of how to care for their bodies, improve muscle strength, enhance flexibility, and maintain physical activities to promote cardiovascular fitness. Strength, flexibility, and cardiovascular fitness are all components of physical well-being and need to be nurtured by the family from the very beginning through the school system and the community.

Sugar

Animals of all kinds have a very strong preference for sugar. In fact, when animals are given sugar, they will reduce their intake of food to increase their consumption of sugar. This is probably because sugar is something that we like from the moment we try it. In fact, it may even be related to the role that sugar has played in our earliest history and our survival. Sweet foods are a quick and easy source of energy. Athletes know this, and so did our earliest ancestors.

Is there any harm in sugar? Many have connected "overdoses" of sugar to a range of problems, from hyperactivity, obesity, and cardiovascular disease to criminal behaviour. There is no compelling research to support these claims. However, excessive consumption of sugar can cause dental caries, particularly when the sugar is consumed steadily. For example, all-day suckers or hard candies which are kept in the mouth for a long time foster the growth of the micro-organisms that are the true guilty parties when it comes to dental caries. The micro-organisms use sugar for their own energy and in doing so create an acid that destroys the enamel of teeth. This allows them to invade the teeth and cause further damage. In order to break the cycle we need to eliminate the source of energy for these bacteria, and the best way of doing that is to brush the teeth after meals and snacks that contain sugar. If tooth brushing is not possible, then certain foods will help clean the teeth. Apples, celery, and other abrasive foods will clear away the sticky sugar and prevent the bacteria from using it.

Foods that are sticky and remain in the teeth also promote the development of the bacteria. These include dried fruits, such as raisins or prunes, as well as peanut butter and jelly sandwiches, which provide hours of energy for the micro-organisms. Therefore, careful food selection as well as oral hygiene can help to reduce the number of dental caries from the time teeth first erupt.

Fortunately for many North American children, fluoride has been added to our water supply and this enables them to develop teeth which are more resistant to decay. Nevertheless, you should keep an eye on your children's consumption of sugar products.

Sugar has been implicated in obesity. However, the true impact of sugar on obesity is hard to assess. Research on the diets of obese children compared to those of average-weight children suggests that their diets do not differ significantly. The main difference between the two groups tends to be the amount of activity in their daily routine. Overweight children are less active than average or underweight ones. This may be a chicken-and-egg issue, however. Are the children overweight because they are less active or are they less active because they are overweight? Certainly encouraging children to enjoy activity and discouraging recreational eating are two positive ways to prevent obesity. And from all the best reports to date, it is clear that prevention is better than treatment. Even so, it is safe to say that a serious effort to restrict sugar is no guarantee for preventing obesity.

Finally, sugar has been linked with hyperactivity in children. It is interesting to note that under experimental conditions, sugar consumption is associated with increased serotonin in the brain. Serotonin is a neurotransmitter (brain messenger) which induces sleep. Researchers have shown that a high sugar intake makes subjects feel sleepy. Research with children who are given sugar has shown that there is no effect on hyperactivity whatsoever. Nevertheless, parents and teachers will claim that when candies are brought into the classroom there is a change in the children's behaviour. This may be more of a social than a physical phenomenon, given the excitement associated with special days and sweet food. Children may feel especially excited to be getting such foods at school or at a birthday party and may react with unusual behaviour. Is it the sugar or the context in which the food is provided?

I recently planned a birthday party for fourteen nine-year-old boys. They played baseball for an hour and then ate cake, ice cream, and chocolate milk. When the parents arrived to retrieve them, they were surprised to find even the most active boys sitting quietly in the backyard. Why? During the last ten minutes of the party I gave out the party favours; each boy got two packs of baseball cards and they were all busy studying their loot and negotiating trades. All the sugar and chocolate caused no reaction at all.

Humans do not have a nutritional need for sugar; it is not an essential requirement. We like sugar and we can use it to enhance the food that we eat. There does not appear to be anything dangerous about consuming a reasonable amount of sugar in foods. Children can eat a certain amount of sweets if they get an adequate amount of all the necessary nutrients in a day and still need additional energy. Try not to make a special fuss over sweet foods so that your children do not come to think of them as rewards or as special activities when they feel bored. Research has shown that when we use sweet foods as a reward, we reinforce children's desires for them.

Supplements

Many parents use multivitamin supplements as a form of insurance to make themselves feel secure that their children have received their share of vitamins each day. But evidence would suggest that this is unnecessary when children eat the recommended intake of foods from all four food groups. Moreover, there are risks associated with overdoses of multivitamin supplements. Because they come in brightly coloured packages and have sweet flavours, children think that they are candies. Every year children are tempted to eat many tablets at once. If you find half a bottle missing, take your child immediately to a hospital to prevent the consequences of overdose.

When do children need supplements? You should recognize the symptoms of malnutrition so that you will know whether your children are getting insufficient nutrients from their food. In North America the most common nutrient deficiencies are iron and calcium. Iron deficiency is most common for children who are consuming a diet that contains little or no meat or iron-fortified bread, grain, or cereals. The iron in meat products is the best because it is very easily absorbed. Fish and seafood, particularly oysters, clams, and mussels, are good sources of iron. However, children are often reluctant to eat meats and it is useful to encourage them to eat breads and cereals which are fortified with iron. Green leafy vegetables such as dark lettuce, spinach, and broccoli also contain a good amount of iron. If you notice symptoms such as constant tiredness, pale membranes around the eyes, or pale tissue under the nail bed, it is time for your child to be evaluated for iron deficiency anemia. One indicator of iron deficiency is that the child may try to eat non-foods such as ice or food from the family pet's dish. These activities are referred to as "pica" and may be indicators of iron deficiency anemia. The desire for ice is a good example of the lack of body wisdom for nutrients. There is no iron in ice and no physiological explanation for this craving. If anemia is diagnosed by the physician, then the child will be placed on iron supplements to ensure adequate iron nutrition.

Research in countries where iron deficiency is high has demonstrated that children's cognitive ability and performance improve when iron is added to their diet. It is estimated that as many as 10 percent of children in the United States and in Canada are iron deficient. It is worth pursuing this issue with your pediatrician or family physician if you have any reason to suspect that your child is iron deficient. But first, look at the typical daily intake of your child to see whether she is getting enough meat or meat alternatives such as lima beans, soya beans, or kidney beans. Other good sources include dried fruits such as peaches, apricots, and prunes. One of our favourite iron-rich foods is a soup made with split peas and beans with added vegetables such as parsley (see page 238). This combination gives children a very good source of iron and makes a nice alternative to sandwiches at lunch time.

To improve the absorption of iron in your child's diet, encourage him to eat foods that contain vitamin C. Vitamin C enhances iron absorption as do natural factors in meat, fish, and poultry. Another excellent way of getting iron into the diet is to cook with an iron skillet. The iron in the cookware actually adds iron to the foods that are prepared in it. Foods that are acidic such as spaghetti sauce or a chili dinner are enhanced dramatically by the use of iron cookware. Although cast iron pots are rather heavy to cook with, they can make a significant contribution to the overall intake of iron by the family.

Calcium is another nutrient of concern, particularly for children and adolescents. During periods of rapid growth, it is important for children to lay down a good bone mass. One of the best sources of calcium is milk, not just because the milk provides calcium but also because milk is fortified with vitamin D which is essential for the absorption of calcium. If children do not like milk there is no harm in adding chocolate powder to get them to drink it. Although chocolate can reduce the absorption of calcium, the small amount added to a cup of milk which is already rich in calcium will not significantly reduce the calcium available to children. The child is far better off drinking milk with some chocolate added than not drinking milk at all.

Other good sources of calcium include the bones of fish such as canned sardines or canned salmon. Shrimp is another good source, along with green vegetables such as broccoli and seeds such as sesame seeds. However, the best source of calcium is milk and dairy products, including cheese, yogurt, and even ice cream. Keep in mind cottage cheese and cream cheese are not very good sources of calcium. Cottage cheese is a reasonable source only when milk liquids are added back to the curds of the cottage cheese.

Children who are lactose intolerant should drink milk that has had the lactose removed from it or take enzymes that help to break down lactose. Young children are not commonly lactose intolerant. The condition usually develops in adolescence. Nevertheless, if your child has gas, bloating, or diarrhea after drinking milk, then it is worth investigating to find out if lactose intolerance is the problem. If this diagnosis is confirmed, get advice from a dietitian. Your child may be able to tolerate small amounts of milk without experiencing any discomfort. She can also get calcium from milk products that have been fermented. Foods such as yogurt as well as hard cheeses such as Swiss, Cheddar, and Muenster are all produced by the action of bacteria which use up the lactose in their own metabolism. It is important to read the labels of yogurt in particular, because some products are simply milk-based blends with some yogurt flavour added to them.

If your child has a real allergy to milk, getting enough calcium may be more difficult, because it is the protein portion of milk to which he reacts and he will not be able to tolerate any milk products. Again, get advice from an experienced dietitian. You can give your child green leafy vegetables such as spinach, turnip greens, broccoli, bok choy, and even tofu to enhance his calcium intake. Children who have a milk allergy should also be evaluated to determine whether a calcium supplement is necessary. Consideration should be given to a vitamin D supplement to go along with it. This decision will be based on how much sunshine children are exposed to. Given our need to protect children from the sun, a vitamin D supplement may be necessary.

Vegetarian Diets for Children

Children raised on vegetarian diets tend to be smaller than their peers who are not. They have no more or fewer colds or childhood illnesses than their peers, but their diet does require some special attention. There are different types of vegetarians. Those who eat fish, milk, and eggs are likely to get a good variety of nutrients. Although iron is best absorbed from meats, with adequate fish, beans, and fortified breads and cereals, these children may not need a supplement. Children who eat no fish or animal-based products whatsoever may not get enough iron, calcium, and vitamin B_{12}. Meal planning for these children should pay special attention to combining grains, legumes, nuts, and seeds to get a good protein intake. A session with a dietitian would be especially worthwhile for parents of strictly vegetarian children. Monitoring their diet and their growth and development would also be a good idea.

Coping with Food Messages in the Media

Television has many different roles to play in shaping children's attitudes towards food and health. Television commercials create demands for foods that are low in nutrients but are promoted as fun to eat, magical to purchase, or valuable to your social life. The messages from television also tell us that successful people are slim yet manage to spend a good part of their day eating and drinking.

Recent studies have shown that there is a significant difference between young couch potatoes and their more active peers in terms of the average degree of obesity. When children are watching television they are physically inactive. At the same time, they are exposed to products that are high in calories and low in nutrients and are likely to eat recreationally. They do not eat because they are hungry but because they need something to do.

Children do not understand that the purpose of television programs is to bring the audience to the advertiser in order to promote a specific product. They need to be educated to be better consumers. As a result of television watching, children often put pressure on their parents to buy the products that they have seen advertised. Shopping for groceries with young children can only lead to embarrassing battles in the supermarket or to regrettable decisions at the cash register. As children get older (around five or six years of age), grocery shopping may provide them with an opportunity to learn about making choices. If they have several requests for breakfast cereals or snacks, let them choose one or two options for that week. As children begin to read and do mathematics, use the shopping trip to reinforce their skills. Ultimately, however, parents need to work with their children to decide which foods will be purchased and served at home. This forms the basic diet for the family. A well-balanced diet based on a variety of healthy foods will help to establish a sound nutritious diet for every member of the family.

CHILDHOOD

RECIPES

THE RECIPES IN THIS SECTION WERE SELECTED WITH THE WHOLE family in mind. Younger and older members of the family need to have foods that are interesting, nutritious, and easy to prepare. The menu planner's worst nightmare is realizing that there are only three recipes that all members of the family enjoy; this leads either to supreme boredom or to the "restaurant syndrome" (everyone has a different meal at the same table). Our goal is to expand your family's repertoire.

In general, children prefer foods that are identifiable (no mysteries allowed), crunchy or crispy in texture, and sweet or bland in taste. These recipes attempt to meet all those demands but we know that it isn't easy. To balance some of the more adventurous recipes, we suggest some simple but familiar accompaniments. It is generally more comforting for children to try one new recipe at a time, especially when it is in the company of some favourite foods.

One great way to get children to try new foods is to involve them in the preparation of the recipes. Watching the ingredients go into a new recipe helps to remove some of the mystery. Try to get the whole family involved in planning the weekly menu. Sit down together once a week and decide as a group what to have for dinner each night. Getting everyone to buy into the plan leaves no surprises for the eaters and no disappointments for the cook.

Depending on their age, activity, and appetite, children are encouraged to select from the minimum number of servings suggested by *Canada's Food Guide to Healthy Eating*. For example, a four-year-old might select five servings of grains throughout the day whereas a twelve-year-old might double that intake. The key is to balance the food groups and select a variety of foods. A typical menu for these two age groups is provided to show how some of these recipes can help you apply the food guide for each child's needs.

	Four-year-old boy	Twelve-year-old girl
Grain products	5 servings	12 servings
Vegetables and fruits	5 servings	10 servings
Milk products	2 servings	4 servings
Meat and alternates	2 servings	3 servings

The guidelines were designed for children four years and older. For younger children, the guidelines can be adapted by reducing the serving sizes by about half. The need for variety is the same but it is most important to match the food intake to the child's appetite. Meals and snacks both contribute to a child's overall nutrient intake. For this reason, we have included some great snack foods to help balance the total day's food plan.

Grain Products

The guidelines recommend 5 to 12 servings of grain products each day. A serving size is defined as one slice of bread, $\frac{2}{3}$ cup (167 mL) of cereal, or $\frac{1}{2}$ cup (125 mL) of pasta or rice. Keep in mind that the total number required daily will depend on each child's needs and appetite. During rapid growth spurts or on very active days, children may have an appetite for more. When growth and activity slow down, so does the appetite. Encourage your child to stay in touch with his energy needs by being aware of his own appetite. Provide a variety of nutritious foods and let him respond to his hunger. Don't force him to eat or make an issue out of it. Let nature take its course.

Most children don't need much encouragement to eat the foods in the grain group. These foods include rice, pasta, breads, ready-to-eat and cooked cereals, muffins, pancakes, and other products made from grains or flours. They provide an important source of starch, fibre, vitamins (thiamin, niacin, and riboflavin), and minerals (iron, zinc, and magnesium).

Incorporate cereals into snack foods such as oatmeal cookies, nuts and bolts, and peanut butter krispies to add grains between meals.

Vegetables and Fruit

Parents often fret over their children's lack of interest in vegetables. When I ask them if they were vegetable lovers as children, the answer is usually no. Further probing often reveals that the child does like certain vegetables and is very fond of fruit. Most kids like fruit and it pays to remember that this food group does include both. There is no reason to force your child to eat vegetables when a glass of orange juice, some carrot sticks, and three other fruits will provide the same nutrients. Add new fruits to the repertoire whenever you can, but always try a sample before introducing a new fruit to your child to make sure that it is at the peak of flavour. An unripe or overripe fruit will increase the chance that they'll never eat that fruit again.

The recommendation for this food group is 5 to 10 servings of fruits and vegetables a day. A serving is one medium-sized fruit or vegetable, 1 cup (250 mL) of salad, or ½ cup (125 mL) of cooked vegetable. Five servings would be reasonable for a younger child and 10 servings for teenagers. These servings can be met with recipes found throughout this section, including soups, frozen fruit juice, and vegetables with dip. We have also hidden vegetables in some of the more adventurous combination foods such as pizza, Vietnamese wrap-ups, and Lazy Gourmet salsa. Think about the foods that your child enjoys most and make them available. Try some of these exciting new recipes when the time seems right and you'll be pleased with the results.

Milk Products

Milk is the sole food for all newborns and continues to be an important source of protein, calcium, and vitamin D for children and adults. Two to three servings are recommended for children aged four to nine years and three to four servings for those aged ten to sixteen. A serving is defined as 1 cup (250 mL) of milk, $\frac{3}{4}$ cup (175 mL) of yogurt, or a 2 oz (50 g) serving of cheese. Discuss problems of lactose intolerance or milk allergy with a dietitian.

This section provides many exciting ways to serve milk products as snacks, soups, or desserts. Try them all.

Meat and Alternatives

The meat and alternatives group includes poultry, meat, fish, legumes, and eggs. This food group is an important source of protein, fat (we all need some!), iron, and B vitamins.

When many of today's parents were growing up, their own parents tended to follow the pattern of "pushing" meats. They were considered valuable sources of protein, and, because of the high cost they added to the grocery bill, no parent could stand to see them go to waste. Fortunately, there are very few documented cases of protein deficiency in Canadian children. In fact, most of them get twice the daily minimum requirement of protein with 2 to 3 servings per day from the meat and alternatives food group and the recommended intake from the milk group. Keep in mind the serving size of 2 to 4 oz (50 to 100 g).

While most children object to one or more of these foods at some point, the group offers a wide range of choices. If your child dislikes the strong flavour of certain meats, try using ground meats in chili or tostados. Most butchers will grind veal, chicken, or pork for an alternative to beef in these recipes.

Try the legume and tofu recipes and remember that peanut butter, on its own or in a sauce, will add to the meat and alternatives food group.

Sauces

We have included various sauces in this section because they add flavour and nutrition to the simplest recipes. Children can acquire a taste for any one of these as easily as they do for ketchup! Whether the sauce is based on peanut butter, beans, or seeds, it is a good source of protein and fibre. All sauces should be kept in the refrigerator.

Try this menu plan to provide the full set of recommended food groups. It is a plan the whole family will enjoy!

Breakfast
juice or fruit
Breakfast Porridge *(p. 225)*
Easy Banana-Walnut Muffin *(p. 228)*
4 oz glass milk

Lunch
Family Fish Chowder *(p. 234)*
fresh rolls
Peanut Butter Krispie *(p. 268)*
sliced green apple

Snack
Oatmeal Cookies *(p. 265)*
Peach Smoothie *(p. 275)*

Dinner
Vietnamese Salad Rolls *(p. 242)*
Lyla's Cranberry Chicken *(p. 257)*
Vegetable Fried Rice with Tofu *(p. 122)*
Butterscotch Pudding *(p. 271)*

Snack
Frozen Fruit Pop *(p. 272)*

Tahini Garlic Dip or Dressing

Tahini is a great non-dairy sauce or dip for vegetables or crackers. Feel free to adjust the garlic to taste.

½ cup (125 mL) tahini

¼ cup (50 mL) lemon juice

½–¾ cup (175 mL) water

2 tsp (10 mL) low-sodium soy sauce

2 cloves garlic, minced

Salt and pepper to taste

Place all ingredients in blender, and blend until creamy.

MAKES 1½ CUPS.

Teriyaki Sauce

This sauce is our family's favourite for salmon. I marinate 1½ lbs (750 g) of salmon for 5 to 10 minutes and then broil or grill the salmon on the barbecue. Now that farmed salmon is available we can enjoy fresh salmon year-round.

1 tbsp (15 mL) minced gingerroot	Mix all ingredients together.
3 cloves garlic, minced	
¾ cup low-sodium soy sauce	
2 tbsp (25 mL) rice wine vinegar or sherry	
1 tsp (5 mL) sesame oil	
1 tbsp (10 mL) brown sugar	

MAKES A LITTLE LESS THAN 1 CUP.

Hoisin Sauce

This is traditionally served as a dipping sauce for cooked meats and salad rolls.

4 tbsp (25 mL) low-sodium soy sauce

4 cloves garlic, minced

4 tbsp (25 mL) hoisin sauce

2 tbsp (15 mL) rice wine vinegar

1 tbsp (10 mL) brown sugar

2 tsp (5 mL) gingerroot, grated

Mix all ingredients together.

MAKES $\frac{2}{3}$ CUP.

Michiko's Miso Sauce

This is the sauce that everyone expects on vegetables when they come to our house for dinner. Miso can be found in Japanese specialty stores and health food stores. It's full of protein and delicious.

½ cup (125 mL) sesame seeds, roasted and ground

7 oz (200 g) mild miso

⅔ cup (150 mL) mirin

2½ tbsp (35 mL) sesame oil

¼ cup (50 mL) sugar

8 to 10 cloves garlic

3 oz (75 g) hot Szechuan paste

¼ cup (50 mL) Japanese rice vinegar

Combine all ingredients in a food processor and process until smooth.

Serve over hot or cold asparagus, green beans, or mixed vegetables. Also great as a dipping sauce.

MAKES 4 CUPS OF SAUCE. KEEPS IN REFRIGERATOR FOR UP TO A MONTH.

Hummus

This Middle Eastern treat is high in protein and fibre. Kids love it at snack time. Great as a dip for pita and hearty breads as well as vegetables.

2 to 3 cloves garlic, minced ¾ cup (175 mL) water ½ tsp (2 mL) salt 2 14-oz (398 mL) cans garbanzo beans, drained 3 tbsp (50 mL) lemon juice	Process all ingredients in food processor for 2 minutes.
½ cup (125 mL) tahini	Gradually add to above and process until thick. (Add more tahini or more water depending on your own desired consistency.)
	MAKES 5 TO 6 CUPS. SERVES 8 TO 10.

Spicy Peanut Sauce No. 1

Try rolling up a flour tortilla with brown rice and peanut sauce and your favourite chopped vegetable.

3 tbsp (50 mL) peanut oil 2 cups (500 mL) chopped onions	Sauté onions in oil until they are brown.
1 bay leaf ¾ tsp (4 mL) cayenne 1 tsp (5 mL) ground coriander seeds	Add and sauté, for 2 to 3 minutes.
2½ cups (625 mL) vegetable stock or water	Add and simmer for 5 minutes.
2 tbsp (25 mL) lemon juice 2 cups (500 mL) peanut butter	Add and simmer for 15 minutes. Stir to avoid burning.
1 to 2 tbsp (15 to 25 mL) brown sugar Salt to taste	Add and stir until sugar is dissolved.
	Delicious over rice or broccoli, or as a vegetable dip. MAKES 5 TO 6 CUPS.

Spicy Peanut Sauce No. 2

This is a versatile sauce for dipping, barbecuing, or pouring over rice and vegetable combinations.

3 tbsp (50 mL) rice vinegar

3 tbsp (50 mL) vegetable oil

2 tbsp (25 mL) low-sodium soy sauce

2 tbsp (25 mL) lime juice

4 tbsp (60 mL) peanut butter

2 tbsp (25 mL) hoisin sauce

1 tbsp (15 mL) sesame oil

1 tsp (5 mL) Chinese chili garlic sauce

4 tbsp (60 mL) water

In saucepan, bring all ingredients to a boil, remove from heat, and simmer 1 minute.

MAKES 1 CUP.

Tzatziki

Tzatziki is a light Mediterranean sauce that's great with everything from raw vegetables to vegetarian burgers.

2 cups (500 mL) plain yogurt	Mix together.
1 tsp (5 mL) minced garlic	
½ cup (125 mL) finely chopped English cucumber	
Salt and pepper to taste	
1 tbsp chopped fresh dill or mint for extra flavour	
	Makes 2 cups.

Bran Muffins

My family picks out the raisins and nuts in muffins so I don't make my muffins with them. However, if your kids like nuts and raisins, add them as the last step before baking.

⅓ cup (75 mL) butter ⅓ cup (75 mL) brown sugar	Cream together.
1 egg, beaten	Add and blend well. Set aside.
1 cup (250 mL) flour 2 tsp (10 mL) baking powder	Sift together.
1½ cups (625 mL) bran cereal	Add to flour.
1 cup (250 mL) buttermilk	Add dry ingredients to brown sugar mixture alternately with buttermilk until all is mixed together. Fill greased muffin tins ⅔ full.
¼ cup (50 mL) raisins (optional) ¼ cup (50 mL) nuts (optional)	These may be added before baking.
	Bake at 400° (200°C) for 20 minutes, or until golden. Makes 1 dozen muffins.

Pumpkin Bread

Pumpkin is a good source of beta-carotene. This bread is a great after-school snack and can be made year-round.

2 cups (500 mL) flour 2 tsp (10 mL) baking powder ¼ tsp (1 mL) salt ¼ tsp (1 mL) cinnamon ¼ tsp (1 mL) ground ginger Pinch ground cloves Pinch grated nutmeg ¼ tsp (1 mL) baking soda	Mix together and set aside.
⅓ cup (75 mL) shortening 1 cup (250 mL) brown sugar	Cream shortening and sugar.
2 eggs	Add one at a time to sugar, beating each time.
1 cup (250 mL) canned pumpkin ¼ cup (50 mL) 2% milk	Add to egg mixture.
	Add dry ingredients to pumpkin mixture and stir until just smooth. Pour into greased loaf pan. Bake in 350° oven for 1 hour, or until tester inserted in centre comes out clean. MAKES 8 SERVINGS.

Oatmeal Pancakes

Pancakes are always a favourite and these have a great texture as well.

1 cup (250 mL) rolled oats 2 cups (500 mL) 2% milk	Soak oats in milk for 10 minutes.
1 egg, beaten ¼ cup (50 mL) vegetable oil	Add to oats and whisk to combine.
1 cup (250 mL) flour 2 tbsp (25 mL) brown sugar 1 tbsp (15 mL) baking powder ½ tsp (2 mL) salt ½ tsp (2 mL) cinnamon	Mix together dry ingredients. Add to oat mixture.
	Heat nonstick skillet over medium heat. Add a little margarine to lightly grease. Drop batter by spoonfuls onto skillet. When bubbles begin to form on surface, then turn and cook until lightly browned. Serve with cinnamon honey butter. SERVES 6.

Cinnamon Honey Butter

Mira loves to make this cinnamon honey butter for breakfast with toast and pancakes. Weekends are a good time for this activity as you have more time to prepare it and clean up.

½ cup (125 mL) soft butter or margarine ½ cup (125 mL) liquid honey 2 to 3 tbsp (50 mL) cinnamon	Mix well. Spread onto pancake.
	Makes 1 cup.

Breakfast Porridge

Oatmeal is a great source of soluble fibre and starch. Kids love oatmeal so get them started when they're young. Brown sugar helps bring out the best in it.

2 cups (500 mL) water ¼ tsp (1 mL) salt	Bring water to a boil in saucepan.
1 cup (250 mL) rolled oats	Add to water. Stir and cook for 1 minute. Reduce heat — cover and cook on low for 15 minutes, or until water is absorbed.
	Sprinkle with brown sugar and serve with cream or milk and fresh fruit. MAKES 3 TO 4 SERVINGS.

To make individual bowls in microwave:

⅔ cup (150 mL) water ⅓ cup (75 mL) rolled oats	Mix together in bowl. Cover bowl with plastic wrap. Cook on High for 1 minute. Stir. Return and cook on High for 30 seconds. Let stand 1 minute in microwave.

Granola for Kids

Get your kids to help you make this easy recipe. They will want to eat it for breakfast every day. Serve it with milk or yogurt and fresh fruit for a complete meal or use it as a topping for ice milk.

5 cups (1.25 L) rolled oats 1 cup (250 mL) wheat germ 1 cup (250 mL) wheat or rye flakes 1 cup (250 mL) raw sunflower seeds, hulled 1 cup (250 mL) unsweetened coconut 1 cup (250 mL) raw almonds, cashews, or walnut pieces ½ cup (125 mL) raw sesame seeds	Mix together.
1 cup (250 mL) liquid honey ½ cup (125 mL) light oil	Combine and add to oat mixture. Stir thoroughly.
	Spread the mixture evenly on a large cookie sheet. Bake at 325°F (160°C) for 10 minutes. Remove from oven and turn mixture to toast other side. Return to oven and repeat process twice. (Entire baking time is approximately 45 minutes.) Mixture should be toasted completely. Cool and add 2 cups (500 mL) raisins. MAKES 3 QTS (3 L).

Oatmeal Blueberry Scones

Serve these warm as an after-school snack with a glass of cold milk.

2 cups (500 mL) flour ½ cup (125 mL) quick-cooking oatmeal ¼ cup (50 mL) sugar 1 tbsp (15 mL) baking powder ½ tsp (2 mL) salt	Mix dry ingredients in bowl.
½ cup (125 mL) butter	Cut into small pieces and add to flour. Mix with fingertips until a coarse meal is formed.
2 eggs, beaten ½ cup (125 mL) light cream	Mix together and add to form dough. Knead for 1 minute.
½ cup (125 mL) fresh or frozen blueberries	Add and mix into dough with a wooden spoon.
	Divide dough into 2 parts. Roll each into a circle ½-inch (1 cm) thick. Cut into 8 wedge-shaped pieces. Place on buttered cookie sheet. Bake even at 425°F (220°C) for 14 to 15 minutes, or until golden. MAKES 16 SCONES.

Easy Banana-Walnut Muffins

This is as easy as it gets! Great for breakfast or send to school for lunch or a snack.

2 cups (500 mL) flour 1 1/2 tsp (7 mL) baking soda	Sift together.
3 eggs, beaten 3 ripe bananas, mashed 1 1/4 cups (375 mL) sugar 1/2 cup (125 mL) vegetable oil 1/2 cup (125 mL) chopped walnuts	Combine thoroughly, then add to flour mixture and stir until just blended.
	Butter muffin tin, or use paper liners. Fill each muffin tin 2/3 full. Bake at 400°F (200°C) for 20 minutes, or until tops of muffins spring back when lightly touched. MAKES ONE DOZEN.

Cornbread

Kids love this served warm with butter or margarine.

1 cup (250 mL) cornmeal ½ cup (125 mL) flour 2 tbsp (25 mL) sugar 1 tbsp (15 mL) baking powder 1 tsp (5 mL) salt	Combine dry ingredients in bowl and mix well.
1 egg, beaten 1½ cups (375 mL) 2% milk	Mix together and add to dry ingredients.
2 tbsp (25 mL) melted butter	Add to cornmeal mixture and mix until blended.
	Pour into 9-inch square (2.5 L) buttered pan. Bake at 375°F (190°C) for 25 to 30 minutes, or until tester inserted in centre comes out clean. SERVES 6.

Raw Vegetables and Dill Dip

Other suggestions for dips include spicy peanut sauce, tahini, hummus, and tzatziki.

Carrot strips Snow peas Broccoli florets Celery stalks Cucumber slices Snap peas Red pepper strips	Wash vegetables well and arrange on a platter.
½ cup (125 mL) mayonnaise ½ cup (125 mL) plain yogurt ½ to 1 tsp (2 to 5 mL) dried dillweed or 1 tbsp (15 mL) fresh dill, chopped ¼ tsp (1 mL) salt Pepper to taste	Mix ingredients together in bowl.
1–2 tbsp ketchup (optional)	Add for a pink sauce.
	MAKES 1 CUP SAUCE.

Nachos

Here is a fun way to serve vegetables without alarming the kids.

10 oz (284 mL) bag tortilla chips 6 oz (150 g) Cheddar cheese, grated	Place 2 to 3 handfuls of tortilla chips onto plate and sprinkle with cheese. Microwave at Medium High for 1 minute, or until cheese has melted. Repeat until all is devoured.
1 cup (250 mL) salsa ½ cup (125 mL) chopped tomatoes ½ cup (125 mL) chopped olives ½ cup (125 mL) chopped cucumbers ½ cup (125 mL) chopped green pepper	Put each into a separate bowl and serve with nachos.
	Serve with 1 cup each guacamole and sour cream.

Lazy Gourmet Salsa

Tomatoes are not always a favourite with children, but for some reason, most kids enjoy salsa. This is a much-coveted recipe from the Lazy Gourmet. The original was given to me by Jane Mundy who caters to the movies in Vancouver. It's always a big hit. Feel free to make it more or less spicy with the jalapeño peppers. It's a good source of vitamin C.

1 14-oz (398 mL) can whole tomatoes

1 14-oz (398 mL) can crushed tomatoes

2 tbsp (25 mL) lemon juice

1 to 2 tbsp (15 to 25 mL) chopped cilantro

2 tsp (10 mL) jalapeño juice

2 jalapeño peppers, chopped

1 small onion, chopped

½ green pepper, chopped

3 or 4 cloves garlic, minced

Combine all ingredients in food processor and process until smooth.

MAKES 4 CUPS SAUCE.

Hearty Vegetable Chowder

Vegetable soup is a wonderful way to boost vegetable eating. Somehow, the kids don't notice how many they've consumed.

1 small onion, chopped fine 2 tbsp (25 mL) butter	Sauté onion in oil for 3 to 4 minutes.
2 carrots, peeled and chopped 1 stalk celery, chopped	Add to onion and cook 5 more minutes.
1 medium potato, peeled and chopped	Add to onion and vegetables.
2 cups (500 mL) water 1 cup (250 mL) frozen corn 1 tsp (5 mL) salt ¼ tsp (1 mL) pepper	Add, cover, and simmer over low heat for 25 minutes.
2 cups (500 mL) 2% milk	Add just before serving and heat thoroughly. Pour into bowls.
1 cup (250 mL) grated Cheddar cheese	Sprinkle each bowl with grated cheese.
	SERVES 4.

Family Fish Chowder

This is a great combination of many of our favourite foods put together into one comfort food for a cold winter's night. Feel free to modify and add your own favourite vegetables and fish.

1 cup (250 mL) chopped onions 3 tbsp (50 mL) butter	Sauté onions in butter until tender.
3 tbsp (50 mL) flour	Add to onions and stir for at least 1 minute.
3 cups (750 mL) 2% milk	Slowly add milk, stirring constantly.
1½ lbs (750 g) halibut, cut into pieces 1 cup (250 mL) vegetable stock 1 cup (250 mL) frozen corn kernels 1 cup (250 mL) frozen peas 8 small new potatoes, chopped 2 carrots, peeled and chopped 2 stalks celery, chopped 1 red pepper, chopped ½ tsp (2 mL) dried marjoram ½ tsp (2 mL) dried basil ½ tsp (2 mL) dried dill 1 tbsp fresh parsley Salt and pepper to taste	Add and simmer for 15 minutes.
	Serves 6.

Mama Rozzie's Chicken Soup with Matzoh Balls

This is the classic Jewish comfort food. It continues to work wonders. Chicken fat used to be credited as the source of "tam" or flavour in Jewish food. Nowadays we let the soup get to room temperature, then skim off the fat and discard it.

2 3-lb (1.5 kg) chicken fryers	Put chickens in large pot and cover with water. Bring to a boil, skim off fat, reduce heat to low, and simmer for 30 minutes. Skim off fat again. Add water to cover and fill pot ⅔ full with water.
8 carrots, washed and halved 3 large white onions, whole 1 bunch celery, cut into 6-inch (15 cm) pieces 1 red pepper, halved 1 tbsp (15 mL) parsley 1 tbsp (15 mL) dill	Add to above and simmer over low heat for about 2 hours, or until chicken is tender.
	Remove chicken and vegetables from pot, and strain liquid through colander with a linen cloth into another pot. Skin and bone chicken, and add meat back to soup. Serve with egg noodles or matzoh balls. SERVES 8, OR 2 PEOPLE WITH COLDS!

Mama Rozzie's Matzoh Balls

We've all been proud of our mother Rozzie's matzoh balls and none of us has yet matched the light texture of them. If the egg whites fall, you might as well plan a baseball game to use up the uneaten balls.

3 egg whites Pinch salt	Beat egg whites with salt until peaks form.
3 egg yolks	Beat well and fold into egg whites.
½ cup (125 mL) matzoh meal	Stir into eggs and let sit in fridge for 2 hours, or until mixture has gone flat.
⅔ pot cold water	Bring water to a boil.
	Wet hands and form the matzoh mixture into small balls the size of walnuts. Drop balls into pot of boiling water, reduce heat to low and simmer for 30 to 40 minutes. Remove with slotted spoon and add to chicken soup. MAKES 8 MATZOH BALLS.

Miso Soup with Tofu

Mira loves to pick out and devour the tofu in this highly nutritious soup; she says it's her favourite soup. Miso can be found in Asian specialty stores. It should be refrigerated at all times. Experiment at home to get the flavour that most suits your family. There are lot of different misos on the market. The darker the colour, the stronger the flavour.

8 cups (2 L) water 1 cup (250 mL) thinly sliced onions 2 medium carrots, cut into thin strips 3 tbsp (50 mL) low-sodium soy sauce 1 1/2 tsp (7 mL) grated gingerroot	Bring water to boil, add vegetables, soy, and ginger, then reduce heat and simmer for 30 minutes.
3 tbsp (50 mL) miso	Remove 1/4 to 1/3 cup (50 to 75 mL) of vegetable broth and add to miso to make into a paste. Return paste to broth. Simmer without boiling for a few minutes longer.
1/2 lb (250 g) tofu, chopped into small pieces	Add and simmer 1 minute longer.
1/2 cup (125 mL) chopped green onion	Sprinkle soup bowls with green onion.
	SERVES 6 TO 8.

Split Pea and Barley Soup

This makes a great meal for a school lunch. Put it in a food jar, add a fresh bagel and a crisp apple, and your kids will sail through the afternoon.

10 cups (2.5 L) water

¾ cup (175 mL) split green peas

¼ cup (50 mL) yellow peas

¼ cup (50 mL) lima beans

¼ cup (50 mL) pearl barley

¼ cup (50 mL) chopped red pepper

2 carrots, chopped

2 stalks celery, chopped

1 onion, chopped

1 large marrow bone or 1 tbsp (15 mL) powdered chicken stock

1 tsp (5 mL) salt

½ tsp (2 mL) pepper

½ tsp (2 mL) turmeric

¼ tsp (1 mL) paprika

2 cloves garlic, minced

Put all ingredients into large pot. Cover and bring to a boil over high heat. Reduce heat to low and simmer for 3 hours.

SERVES 8.

Chappati Roll-Ups

This is a variation of the one of the hottest new items on the market for healthful eating in Vancouver. Play with varieties of vegetables and sauces. Pesto sauce adds an Italian flavour and salsa adds a Mexican flavour.

6 chappatis or rotis 4 cups (1 L) cooked brown rice, warm	Place ⅔ cup (150 mL) brown rice along bottom of each chappati, leaving 2 inches (5 cm) of chappati on each side to be folded over.
2 cups (500 mL) grated carrots 1 cup (250 mL) grated red pepper 1 cup (250 mL) mung bean sprouts 1 cup (250 mL) chopped spinach leaves	Top rice with ⅙ of each of the vegetables.
¾ to 1 cup (175 to 250 mL) Spicy Peanut Sauce	Pour 2 to 3 tbsp (25 to 50 mL) of peanut sauce on top. Fold over sides of chappati and roll up.
	MAKES 6.

Tomato and Cheese Strata

Notice how there is nothing in here that the kids are likely to complain about. Feel free to use a canned tomato sauce instead of the fresh tomato sauce.

1 tbsp (15 mL) butter 1 tbsp (25 mL) olive oil 1 medium onion, chopped	Sauté onion in butter and oil until translucent.
4 cups (1 L) tomatoes, peeled, seeded, and chopped 3 cloves garlic, minced Bay leaf	Add to onion and cook for about 20 minutes, or until sauce is a chunky purée. Discard bay leaf. Run sauce through food processor or blender.
1 day-old French loaf 3 cups (750 mL) 2% milk	Grease 9 x 13-inch (3.5 L) casserole. Cut bread into 27 pieces. Dip bread into milk to soften.
½ lb (250 g) mozzarella, thinly sliced ½ lb (250 g) fontina cheese, thinly sliced	Arrange 9 slices of bread on bottom of casserole.
6 eggs, beaten well	Spread 1 cup (250 mL) tomato sauce on top. Arrange half the cheese over sauce. Repeat with another layer of bread, sauce, and cheese. Top with last 9 slices of bread and remaining sauce.
3 to 4 tbsp (50 to 60 mL) grated Parmesan cheese 1 tbsp (15 mL) butter	Pour eggs over casserole, piercing bread with tip of knife until eggs are absorbed. Sprinkle with Parmesan and dot with butter. Let stand ½ hour, or until eggs are absorbed.
	Bake at 375°F (190°C) for about 45 minutes, or until set. SERVES 8 TO 10.

Cheese Quesadillas

Rena makes her quesadillas with 1 tbsp (15 mL) of pesto and 2 oz (50 g) low-fat Monterey Jack cheese between two tortillas. She then puts the quesadilla into an ungreased skillet, and heats it on medium for three minutes on each side until the cheese is melted and the tortilla is crispy. A delicious lunch with a tossed salad. Experiment and try your favourite fillings. Use leftovers, or ask your kids what they would like in their quesadillas. It's a great change from the traditional grilled cheese sandwich!

10 5-inch (12 cm) flour tortillas 1 egg, beaten	Place five tortillas on counter. Brush each on open side with egg.
2 cups (500 mL) grated Swiss cheese 1 cup (250 mL) light cream cheese ½ purple onion, chopped ½ red pepper, chopped fine 1 jalapeño pepper, seeded, then chopped fine (optional)	Mix all ingredients for filling together.
	Spread ⅕ of filling on top of each tortilla. Place another tortilla on top of cheese mixture. Press gently. Brush remaining egg on top and press around edges to seal. Bake in 350°F (180°C) oven for about 10 minutes, or until golden. Remove from oven. Let sit 3 minutes, then cut into triangles. Serve with salsa.

Vietnamese Salad Rolls

This recipe was originally given to me by South China Seas Food Shop in Granville Island Market. Most rice paper is imported from Thailand. You can find it in many Asian food stores. When removed from the package, the papers curl up, so keep them wrapped before you use them.

6 to 8 oz (175 to 225 g) rice vermicelli	Bring pot of water to a boil. Add vermicelli, turn off heat, and let noodles soak for 5 minutes. Rinse with water and drain. Set aside.
8 pieces of rice paper	Fill a large bowl with warm water. Immerse one sheet of rice paper in the water for 5 seconds, or until softened. Remove to plate. Fold over the bottom ⅓ of the paper.
8 to 12 lettuce leaves	Put one or two lettuce leaves on the folded paper and put about 1 oz (25 g) vermicelli on top. Fold up slightly.
1 cup (250 mL) grated carrot 8 oz (200 g) cooked shrimp or cooked chicken	Put about 2 tbsp (25 mL) of carrots and 1 oz (25 g) shrimp or chicken on the lettuce.
8 green onions, trimmed	Add the green onion in front of the vermicelli so that it will protrude from the finished roll. Roll the folded bottom edge away from you, enveloping the ingredients and making a tight roll. Repeat with the remaining sheets. Keep in a cool, moist place until serving time. Serve with satay sauce or hoisin sauce.
	MAKES 8 ROLLS.

Chicken, Shrimp, and Beef Satays with Peanut Sauce

This food is fun to eat and kids should also have a variety of sauces for dipping. It makes everyone feel as if they're in a restaurant and it's not much effort.

36 bamboo skewers	Soak the skewers in water for 30 minutes (prevents burning on barbecue and slivers in the mouth).
1 cup (250 mL) low-sodium soy sauce 3 tbsp (50 mL) grated gingerroot 3 tbsp (50 mL) sherry 3 tbsp (50 mL) fresh lime juice 2 tbsp (25 mL) brown sugar 4 cloves garlic, minced	Combine in glass dish. Divide into 3 small bowls.
24 uncooked shrimp, shelled 1 lb (500 g) boneless chicken breasts, cut into ½-inch (1 cm) wide strips 1 lb (500 g) beef steak, cut into 3 x ½-inch (7.5 x 1 cm) strips	Marinate shrimp, beef, and chicken separately in the 3 bowls; cover and chill for 30 minutes.
	Thread shrimp, chicken, and beef on separate skewers. Grill about 3 minutes on each side. Chicken takes a little longer, shrimp will be done when curled and pink. Serve with peanut sauce, hoisin sauce, and tahini. MAKES 36 SKEWERS.

Peanut Sauce

This sauce is more popular than ketchup.

1 cup (250 mL) creamy (not old-fashioned) peanut butter

1 14-oz (398 mL) can low-sodium chicken or vegetable broth

$\frac{1}{4}$ cup (50 mL) lime juice

3 tbsp (50 mL) brown sugar

$2\frac{1}{2}$ tbsp (45 mL) low-sodium soy sauce

2 tbsp (25 mL) grated gingerroot

$\frac{1}{2}$ to 1 tsp (2 to 5 mL) chili garlic oil or $\frac{1}{2}$ tsp (2 mL) dried crushed red pepper

Stir well in saucepan and cook over medium heat for 6 to 8 minutes, or until smooth.

MAKES 3 CUPS.

Stuffed Baked Potatoes

A great comfort food lunch for kids who come home from school and a good way to use up leftover chicken or potatoes from the night before.

4 large potatoes	Bake potatoes in 350°F (180°C) oven for 1 hour, or until soft inside. Cut in half and scoop out potato into bowl.
4 tbsp (60 mL) butter ¾ cup (175 mL) grated cheese	Add to potato in bowl.
1 to 2 tbsp (15 to 25 mL) 2% milk	Add enough milk to soften mixture.
½ cup (125 mL) chopped chicken, cooked ½ cup (125 mL) frozen peas, thawed	Add to potato mixture. Stuff potato skins with mixture. Return to oven for 15 minutes.
	SERVES 4.

Variations for Stuffed Potatoes

Pizza Filling	Mix 4 oz (100 g) chopped salami, 6 oz grated mozzarella cheese, and 2 tbsp grated Parmesan cheese into potato mixture. Top with 1 cup tomato sauce.
Taco filling	Mix ½ of a 19 oz can red kidney beans, ½ cup (125 mL) grated Cheddar cheese, ½ cup (125 mL) sour cream, and ¼ cup (50 mL) crushed taco chips into potato mixture. Top with 1 cup salsa.

Mama Rozzie's Green Bean Casserole

It's kind of old-fashioned, but it was the only way Mom could get us to eat green beans.

2 lbs (1 kg) frozen green beans 1 10-oz (284 mL) can cream of mushroom soup	Mix together beans and soup. Turn into buttered 9 x 13-inch (3.5 L) casserole.
1 can French fried onion rings	Top with onion rings. Bake at 350°F (180°C) for 30 to 35 minutes.
	MAKES 1 9 x 13-INCH CASSEROLE.

Tuna Pineapple Pita Pockets

Pita pockets are fun for school lunches and can be filled with your child's favourite vegetables, meat, and cheeses.

1 4-oz (113 g) can tuna, drained 1 8-oz can crushed pineapple, drained ¼ cup (50 mL) shredded cabbage 2 oz (50 g) Cheddar cheese, grated 2 tbsp (25 mL) mayonnaise	Mix all ingredients together.
8 pitas	Fill pita pockets with tuna mixture. Place in casserole dish and cover. Bake in oven at 325°F (160°C) for 15 minutes, or until centres are warm, or microwave, uncovered, for 90 seconds on High.
	MAKES 8 PITA POCKETS.

Easy Pita Pizzas

This is a delightful way to include the family in preparing their own meals. Pita pizzas are easy and nutritious.

4 whole wheat pitas 1 cup (250 mL) tomato sauce	Put ¼ cup (50 mL) of sauce on top of each pita.
2 tomatoes, sliced ½ red pepper, chopped ½ green pepper, chopped 8 slices salami or pepperoni 8 slices turkey	Let each family member add his or her own toppings.
6 to 8 oz (150 to 200 g) mozzarella cheese, grated ¼ cup (50 mL) grated Parmesan cheese	Top each pizza with cheese.
	Put pizzas on baking sheet. Bake at 450°F (230°C) for 10 minutes, or until bubbly. MAKES 4 PIZZAS.

Beef Tostadas on Tortillas

These can be a bit messy, but that's part of the fun!

1 tbsp (15 mL) olive oil ¼ cup (50 mL) finely chopped onion	Sauté onion in oil until translucent.
1 lb (500 g) ground beef or refried beans	Add beef or beans to onion and stir until cooked completely. Drain off excess fat.
⅓ cup (75 mL) chili sauce	Add to meat or bean mixture and stir.
8 corn tortillas	Heat tortillas in oven at 350°F (180°C) for 5 minutes, or until warm. Spoon ⅛ of meat or bean mixture onto each tortilla.
2 tomatoes, chopped ½ head lettuce, chopped into strips 6 oz (150 g) Cheddar cheese, grated 1 cup (250 mL) salsa	Use as toppings for each tortilla. Roll up.
	MAKES 8 TORTILLAS.

Fettucine Lasagna

This is one of the most popular items for sale at the Lazy Gourmet. It's much easier and faster to make than traditional lasagnas, but every bit as delicious.

3 1/2 cups (875 mL) tomato sauce	Use canned sauce or make your own.
1 1/2 lbs (750 g) fresh or 1 lb (500 g) dry fettucine	Cook pasta in boiling water for 5 to 6 minutes for fresh pasta; 8 to 10 minutes for dry. Set aside.
4 oz (100 g) mozzarella cheese, grated 4 oz (100 g) Swiss cheese, grated 1/2 cup (125 mL) grated Parmesan cheese	Mix cheeses together. Divide into two portions. Set aside.
2 eggs, beaten 1 1/2 cup (375 mL) ricotta cheese Pinch nutmeg Salt and pepper to taste	Mix together and set aside.
	In large bowl, combine tomato sauce, noodles, and one portion of cheese mixture. Put half of this mixture into 9 x 13-inch (3.5 L) casserole dish. Spoon egg mixture over noodles. Top with remaining tomato, cheese, and pasta mixture and sprinkle with second portion of cheese mixture. Bake at 30 to 35 minutes at 350°F (180°C), or until bubbly. MAKES 1 9 x 13-INCH CASSEROLE. SERVES 8.

Quick Tomato Sauce

*This is a quick and easy way to make a delicious tomato sauce.
Use it for any kind of pasta, tacos, or chili.*

1 to 2 tbsp (15 mL) olive oil 1 onion, chopped	In large saucepan, sauté onion in oil for 4 to 5 minutes.
3 cloves garlic, minced	Add to onion and sauté for about 30 seconds.
½ cup (125 mL) water 2 carrots, grated 1 19-oz can crushed tomatoes 3 tbsp (50 mL) tomato paste 1 tsp (5 mL) dried basil ¼ tsp (1 mL) oregano Pinch dried thyme	Add and cook for 30 minutes. Purée in blender.
	MAKES 2 CUPS.

Quick and Simple Chili Con Carne

Kids seem to love this recipe.

1 tbsp (15 mL) vegetable oil 1 lb (500 g) ground beef or pork 2 cloves garlic, minced	In large skillet, sauté beef and garlic in oil until thoroughly cooked. Drain off excess fat.
1 14-oz (398 mL) can red kidney beans, drained 1½ cups (375 mL) tomato sauce ¼ cup (50 mL) tomato paste 1 tsp (4 to 5 mL) chili powder	Add to meat and cook over medium heat for 20 to 25 minutes.
	Serve with corn chips or corn bread.

Easy and Delicious Tuna Casserole

This casserole is chock full of ingredients that kids like to eat, so you're not likely to find bits picked out. It's an old-fashioned recipe, but kids seem to love it. It can be made ahead and reheated or you can make a double batch and freeze half.

Ingredients	Instructions
3 cups (750 mL) cooked macaroni noodles 3 cups (750 mL) grated cheese 1 10-oz (284 mL) can cream of mushroom soup 1 cup (250 mL) frozen peas 1 cup (250 mL) chopped celery 1 7½-oz can tuna, drained ½ cup (125 mL) 2% milk ½ tsp (2 mL) salt ½ tsp (2 mL) pepper	Mix all ingredients together. Pour into 9 x 13-inch casserole dish.
1 cup (250 mL) cornflake crumbs 2 tbsp (25 mL) melted butter	Mix together crumbs and butter. Spread evenly on top of casserole.
	Bake at 350°F (180°C) for 30 minutes, or until bubbly. SERVES 8.

Crispy Fish Fillets

Kids like crispy foods and this is one way to get them excited about fish.

6 snapper, cod, or halibut fillets 2 eggs, beaten Pinch each salt and pepper	Dip fillets into seasoned eggs.
1 cup (250 mL) cornflake or bread crumbs	Coat fillets with crumbs.
2 to 3 tbsp (50 mL) vegetable oil	Fry fillets in oil for 3 minutes on each side, or until golden brown.
	Serve with wedges of lemon and Cucumber and Dill Sauce. MAKES 6 FILLETS.

Cucumber and Dill Sauce

This is a light flavourful sauce that kids love for dipping or as a condiment.

1 cup (250 mL) plain yogurt 1/3 cup (75 mL) grated English cucumber 1/2 tsp (2 mL) fresh dill 1/4 tsp (1 mL) salt	Mix together and serve with fish.

Our Family's Favourite Chicken

This is everyone's favourite chicken dish. Mira has been helping me make it since she was two years old. She knows that she's not allowed to put her fingers into her mouth when working with food. I rarely tell anyone at the time how easy this recipe is as I always get rave reviews for it. Sometimes I use a garlic-based dressing, but recently I've tried dressings with sun-dried tomatoes and other more exotic foods and everyone loves it.

1 chicken, skinned and cut up ½ bottle (8 oz) salad dressing, any kind	Coat chicken in salad dressing.
¾ to 1 cup (175 to 250 mL) cornflake crumbs	Dip chicken pieces into crumbs one at a time and place in roasting pan. Bake at 375°F (190°C) for 1 hour, or until chicken is tender.
	SERVES 4 TO 6.

Lyla's Cranberry Chicken

A Friday-night special year-round. Lyla has become famous nationwide for this recipe. It was originally published in my official Expo 86 souvenir cookbook and in sister Lynnie's runaway best seller, Chicken! Chicken! Chicken!

1 14-oz (398 mL) can whole cranberry sauce ⅓ cup (75 mL) honey ¼ cup (50 mL) orange juice concentrate ¼ cup (50 mL) low-sodium soy sauce	Combine ingredients in medium saucepan and bring to boil. Reduce heat and simmer for 5 minutes.
4 lb (2 kg) chicken, skinned and cut into serving pieces	Pour sauce over chicken and bake at 375°F (190°C) for 1 hour. Turn occasionally. The longer you cook it, the stickier it gets.
	SERVES 4 TO 6.

Pizza Dough

With a pizza dough recipe, you can make great individual pizzas any time. Feel free to add herbs and cheese to make a simple foccacio bread.

1⅓ cups (325 mL) warm water 1 tbsp (15 mL) sugar	Dissolve sugar in warm water.
1 package dry yeast	Add yeast to sugared water and let stand for 10 minutes.
3 cups (750 mL) flour 2 tbsp (25 mL) vegetable oil 1 tsp (5 mL) salt	Stir into yeast mixture to form dough. Knead until smooth and elastic.
	Place dough in oiled bowl and turn to coat all surfaces. Cover with oiled wax paper and let sit in warm place for 1 hour, or until doubled. Punch down and stretch to fit 14-inch (35 cm) pizza pan or cookie sheet. Top with your favourite sauce (tomato or pesto) and your favourite cheeses and toppings. Bake at 400°F (200°C) for 20 minutes, or until bubbly. MAKES ONE 14-INCH (35 CM) PIZZA CRUST.

Whole Wheat Pizza Dough

Whole wheat pizza has a heartier texture but one feels morally superior for making it!

1 ¼ cups (300 mL) warm water 1 tsp (5 mL) sugar	Dissolve sugar in warm water.
1 package dry yeast	Add yeast to sugared water and let stand for 5 minutes.
1 ¼ cups (300 mL) white flour 1 ¼ cups (300 mL) whole wheat flour 1 tsp (5 mL) salt	Mix together.
5 tbsp (75 mL) vegetable oil	Combine yeast mixture, flour, and oil. Knead until smooth and elastic. If dough sticks to bowl, add a bit more flour; if it's too dry, add some water, 1 tsp (5 mL) at a time.
	Transfer dough to greased bowl and turn to coat all sides with oil. Cover and let stand in a warm spot for 1 hour, or until doubled in volume. Punch down and stretch to fit 14-inch (35 cm) pizza pan or cookie sheet. Note: After the dough has risen, you can refrigerate it up to three days. MAKES ONE 14-INCH (35 CM) PIZZA CRUST.

Fantasy Party Pizzas

Pizzas are the ultimate application of the food guide! You can combine all four food groups into one delicious and nutritious serving.

2 cups (500 mL) grated cheese, any kind 1 cup (250 mL) tomato sauce	Spread cheese and tomato sauce on pizza crust.
Red peppers, chopped Green peppers, chopped Mushrooms, sliced Tomatoes, sliced Pineapple, chopped Pepperoni or salami, sliced Sun-dried tomatoes, chopped Eggplant, sliced Olives	Let the children choose their own toppings.
	Bake in 425°F (220°C) oven on bottom rack for about 15 minutes, or until bubbly. MAKES 1 PIZZA.

Pizza Sauce

The longer you cook this, the thicker the sauce will be. Just make sure to stir so it doesn't burn.

2 tbsp (25 mL) olive oil	Heat oil in saucepan.
2½ lbs (1.25 kg) fresh tomatoes, chopped	Add to oil and sauté.
¼ cup (50 mL) tomato paste 1 small carrot, grated 2 tbsp (25 mL) minced fresh basil or 1 tsp (5 mL) dried basil 1 tsp (5 mL) sugar ½ tsp (2 mL) thyme ½ tsp (2 mL) oregano ½ tsp (2 mL) red pepper flakes 1 clove garlic, minced Salt and pepper to taste	Add vegetables, sugar, and herbs to tomatoes and cook, stirring occasionally, for 35 to 45 minutes.
	MAKES 1½ TO 2 CUPS.

Pesto Sauce

Basil and parsley are loaded with beta-carotene, vitamin C, and other vitamins. Use this sauce on pastas, pizzas, or quesadillas and in soups. Your kids are sure to love it.

3 cups (750 mL) fresh basil leaves 1 cup (250 mL) fresh parsley sprigs 4 cloves garlic, minced ½ cup (125 mL) grated Parmesan cheese ½ cup (125 mL) toasted pine nuts or walnuts	Using blender or food processor, process until ingredients are thoroughly mixed.
1 cup (250 mL) olive oil	Add oil to herb mixture gradually, continuing to process, until a creamy paste is formed.
Freshly ground pepper Salt	Add to taste.
	Makes 1½ to 2 cups.

Four-Cheese Pizza

Feel free to experiment with any four cheeses. This was our favourite combo.

Dough for 14-inch (35 cm) pizza	Bake at 475°F (240°C) for 20 minutes, or until bubbly.
2 oz (50 g) mozzarella cheese, grated 2 oz (50 g) Camembert (include rind) 2 oz (50 g) Parmesan cheese, grated 2 oz (50 g) feta cheese, crumbled	Mix together.
1 cup (250 mL) tomato sauce	Spread sauce over crust. Top with cheeses. Bake at 475°F (240°C) for 20 minutes, or until bubbly.
	SERVES 2 TO 4.

Nuts and Bolts Mix

Great to keep around the house for a nutritious snack.

3 cups (750 mL) bite-sized shredded wheat cereal

3 cups (750 mL) Cheerios or 2 cups (500 mL) thin pretzels, broken into smaller pieces

2 cups (500 mL) roasted peanuts

Mix together and keep in jars for quick snacks.

MAKES 7 TO 8 CUPS (1.75 TO 2 L).

Oatmeal Cookies

Feel free to add carob or chocolate chips, coconut, or walnuts.

¾ cup (175 mL) brown sugar ½ cup (125 mL) margarine	Cream sugar and margarine well.
1 egg, beaten	Add to sugar and margarine.
½ cup (125 mL) 2% milk	Add to egg mixture. Set aside.
2 cups (500 mL) flour 1 tsp (5 mL) baking soda ½ tsp (2 mL) salt	Sift flour, soda, and salt into bowl. Combine with egg mixture and mix well.
2 cups (500 mL) rolled oats 1 cup (250 mL) raisins	Add to flour mixture and stir well.
	Drop by teaspoons onto cookie sheets. Bake at 350°F (180°C) for 12 minutes, or until golden brown. MAKES 3 DOZEN COOKIES.

Peanut Butter and Honey Granola Bars

This is a snack loaded with fibre, vitamins, and minerals.

3 cups (750 mL) rolled oats 1 cup (250 mL) bran 1 cup (250 mL) unsweetened coconut 1 cup (250 mL) sunflower seeds ½ cup (125 mL) chopped almonds (optional) ½ cup (125 mL) raisins ¼ cup (50 mL) wheat germ	Mix dry ingredients in large bowl. Set aside.
½ cup (125 mL) honey ½ cup (125 mL) vegetable oil ½ cup (125 mL) brown sugar ½ cup (125 mL) peanut butter	Combine in small saucepan and cook over medium-low heat until dissolved.
1 tbsp (15 mL) 2% milk 2 tsp (10 mL) vanilla ¾ tsp (4 mL) baking soda	Combine and add to honey mixture. Bring to a boil, then remove from heat.
	Pour honey-milk mixture over granola mixture and stir well. Wet your hands and press mixture into 15 x 10-inch (2 L) jelly roll pan. Bake at 275°F (140°C) for 20 to 25 minutes. Cut into slices and store in refrigerator. MAKES 2 QTS.

Apple Crisp

This is an all-time favourite. Your kids will love to help make this crunchy dessert.

6 large apples, peeled and sliced	Arrange apples in 9-inch square (2.5 L) greased pan.
¼ cup (50 mL) water 1 tbsp (15 mL) lemon juice 1 tbsp (15 mL) cinnamon ½ tsp (2 mL) cloves	Mix together and sprinkle over apples. Set aside.
¾ cup (175 mL) flour ¾ cup (175 mL) brown sugar ½ cup (125 mL) rolled oats 6 tbsp (90 mL) butter	Rub together to form crumbs. Spread over apples.
	Bake at 350°F (180°C) for 35 to 40 minutes. Serve hot or cold. SERVES 6 TO 8.

Peanut Butter Krispies

*Lots of nutrition packed into a great snack. These could last a
week if stored in an airtight container.*

1 cup (250 mL) corn syrup 1 cup (250 mL) brown sugar	Heat syrup and sugar in small saucepan until sugar is dissolved.
1 cup (250 mL) peanut butter	Add peanut butter to sugar mixture and stir until bubbles form.
3 cups (750 mL) Special K cereal 3 cups (750 mL) Rice Krispies	Add to peanut butter mixture and stir well.
	Press into lightly oiled 9 x 13-inch (3.5 L) pan. Chill for 30 minutes before cutting into 24 squares. MAKES 24 SQUARES.

Snack Kit

Take small amounts at a time in small bags for a quick energy snack. It's also a great snack for adults!

2 cups (500 mL) toasted nuts, any kind

1 cup (250 mL) sunflower seeds

1 cup (250 mL) dried prunes, apricots, and peaches

$\frac{1}{2}$ cup (125 mL) raisins

$\frac{1}{2}$ cup (125 mL) carob chips

$\frac{1}{2}$ cup (125 mL) coconut

Mix together and store in a tightly covered jar.

MAKES 5$\frac{1}{2}$ CUPS.

Rice Pudding

This recipe brings together three of the food groups. Add fruit and you've got them all.

4 cups (1 L) whole or 2% milk 1 cup (125 mL) long-grain rice ½ cup (125 mL) sugar ½ tsp (2 mL) salt ¼ tsp (1 mL) cinnamon Pinch nutmeg	Put into large saucepan. Cover and cook over low heat for 2 hours. Stir every 15 minutes.
2 egg yolks 2 tbsp (25 mL) water 1 tsp (5 mL) vanilla	Mix together egg yolks, water, and vanilla. Add 1 cup (250 mL) rice mixture to egg mixture. Return to pot and cook additional 4 to 5 minutes.
3 to 4 tbsp (60 mL) sugar 1 tbsp (15 mL) cinnamon	Combine well. Pour on top of pudding. Serve warm.
	SERVES 4.

Butterscotch Pudding

Kids will love to help you make this recipe and, of course, lick the spoon afterwards!

1 cup (250 mL) light brown sugar 2 tbsp (25 mL) cornstarch ¼ tsp (1 mL) salt	Combine in medium saucepan over medium heat.
2 cups (500 mL) whole or 2% milk	Whisk in gradually. Cook 15 minutes, or until thick and bubbly.
2 egg yolks	In separate bowl, beat yolks. Add ½ cup (125 mL) milk mixture to yolks and stir. Add this mixture to saucepan and cook an additional 2 minutes.
1 tbsp (15 mL) butter 1 tsp (5 mL) vanilla	Remove from heat and add butter and vanilla. Stir until butter has melted.
	Pour pudding into serving bowl. Cover with plastic wrap to prevent skin from forming. Let cool 1 hour before serving. SERVES 4

Frozen Banana Pops

This is an obvious way to get your children involved in preparing a nutritious snack. It's easy to make and lots of fun to eat.

2 ripe bananas, peeled and cut in half 4 tbsp (60 mL) shredded coconut	Roll bananas in coconut.
	Carefully put popsicle stick into bananas. Wrap each pop in waxed paper, and freeze for at least 2 to 3 hours (overnight is better). MAKES 4 POPS.

Frozen Fruit Pops

1 ½ tsp (7 mL) unflavoured gelatin 2 cups (500 mL) fruit juice	Sprinkle gelatin over ½ cup (125 mL) fruit juice in small saucepan. Let stand 2 minutes. Stir over low heat until gelatin dissolves. Add remaining fruit juice and stir well. Remove from heat.
	Pour into popsicle moulds and freeze for 3 hours, or until firm. MAKES 6 TO 8 POPS.

Everyday Frozen Pops

A kid's favourite to eat and to help make. It's a good idea to make them early in the day so that you will be able to enjoy them the same day.

2 cups (500 mL) fruit-flavoured yogurt 2 cups (500 mL) 2% milk	Combine and stir well.
	Pour into popsicle moulds. Put sticks into yogurt. Freeze overnight. MAKES EIGHT 4-OZ (100 G) POPS.

Easy Frozen Juice Pops

1 12-oz (341 mL) can frozen fruit juice 2 cans water	Dilute concentrated juice with water. Pour into popsicle moulds and freeze 1 hour or until partially set. Put sticks into moulds. Freeze overnight.
	MAKES 16 POPS.

Frozen Pudding Sticks

4 oz (113 g) package instant pudding 4 cups (1 L) 2% milk, heated until very hot	Combine and stir well. Let return to room temperature.
	Pour pudding into popsicle moulds. When partially frozen add sticks. Freeze overnight. MAKES 16 POPS.

Milk Shakes

Add fruit to milk shakes for extra flavour and nutrition.

2 scoops ice milk 1 cup (250 mL) cold 2% milk	Put milk and ice milk in blender and blend well. Pour into tall glass.
¼ cup (50 mL) blueberries ¼ cup (50 mL) raspberries ¼ cup (50 mL) strawberries ½ banana	Add any of these for a fruity flavour and blend.

Banana Smoothie

Healthful snacks encourage good eating habits. It's a great snack for moms because it's full of calcium.

1 banana 1 cup (250 mL) 2% milk 1 cup (250 mL) ice cubes ½ tsp (2 mL) vanilla 2 tsp (10 mL) honey	Process in blender until smooth.

Peach Smoothie

1 cup (250 mL) canned peaches, drained 1 cup (250 mL) ice cubes 1 cup (250 mL) vanilla yogurt ½ cup (125 mL) orange juice	Process in blender until smooth.

Mixed Fruit Smoothie

1 cup (250 mL) fruit yogurt 1 cup (250 mL) ice cubes ½ cup (125 mL) fresh raspberries 1 ripe peach ½ banana	Process in blender until smooth.

Party Sandwiches

Everyone loves party sandwiches but most people find them a pain to make. Get your kids to help and have them make up a big batch together on the weekend. Freeze them and let them choose each day which ones they want to take to school. Here are some great ideas for fillings and variations. It'll be a party for you all week!

Roll-up sandwiches
Ask the baker to slice your whole wheat and enriched white bread lengthwise. When you have your filling ready, use a rolling pin to gently press the bread down. This will make it easier to roll up and you will not tear the bread. Spread with filling and roll up tightly. Wrap with plastic wrap and chill overnight or freeze until ready to cut. Cut them at the last minute, as the bread tends to go stale quickly.

Ribbon sandwiches
Spread a slice of white bread with tuna, top with a slice of whole wheat bread, spread egg salad on the whole wheat slice, and top with another slice of white bread. Chill and cut into strips.

Triangle sandwiches
Use one kind of bread on the bottom and another on the top. Fill them and cut them into small triangles.

Cut-out sandwiches
These are cute and great for parties, but can be wasteful if much of the sandwich is left out of the cutter. If you can find good cutters that will use most of the sandwich, go ahead and have fun with them. We have a Mickey Mouse cutter that looks great and ensures minimal waste.

Sandwich Fillings and Spreads

In addition to the usual standbys of peanut butter and jelly, peanut butter and banana, sliced cheese, or sliced meat, try these fillings. Always serve with vegetable sticks and dips.

Egg salad
3 hard-cooked eggs
2 tbsp (25 mL) mayonnaise
Salt and pepper to taste

Homemade cheese spread
½ cup (125 mL) cream cheese
1 cup (250 mL) grated Cheddar cheese

Pineapple cheese spread
½ cup (125 mL) cream cheese
½ cup (125 mL) crushed pineapple

Tuna or salmon salad
7½ oz (213 mL) can tuna or salmon
4 tbsp (25 mL) mayonnaise
2 tbsp (15 mL) toasted sunflower seeds (optional)
2 tsp (5 mL) lemon juice

Party Pita Pockets

Pita pockets are a big hit at parties. Have the pitas pre-cut so that the kids can see the pockets. Put a variety of fillings on the table and let the kids fill up the pocket with their favourites. Don't have too many different choices—it will only confuse them.

Sliced or chopped or grated cheeses
Sliced tomatoes
Shredded lettuce
Chopped cucumbers
Egg salad
Tuna salad
Peanut butter and jam
Hummus and tahini

Canada's Food Guide
to Healthy Eating

CANADA'S
Food Guide
TO HEALTHY EATING
FOR PEOPLE FOUR YEARS AND OVER

Different People Need Different Amounts of Food

The amount of food you need every day from the 4 food groups and other foods depends on your age, body size, activity level, whether you are male or female and if you are pregnant or breast-feeding. That's why the Food Guide gives a lower and higher number of servings for each food group. For example, young children can choose the lower number of servings, while male teenagers can go to the higher number. Most other people can choose servings somewhere in between.

Grain Products
5-12
SERVINGS PER DAY

1 Serving
1 Slice
Cold Cereal — 30 g
Hot Cereal — 175 mL — 3/4 cup

2 Servings
1 Bagel, Pita or Bun
Pasta or Rice — 250 mL — 1 cup

Vegetables & Fruit
5-10
SERVINGS PER DAY

1 Serving
1 Medium Size Vegetable or Fruit
Fresh, Frozen or Canned Vegetables or Fruit — 125 mL — 1/2 cup
Salad — 250 mL — 1 cup
Juice — 125 mL — 1/2 cup

Milk Products
SERVINGS PER DAY
Children 4-9 years: 2-3
Youth 10-16 years: 3-4
Adults: 2-4
Pregnant & Breast-feeding Women: 3-4

1 Serving
MILK — 250 mL — 1 cup
Cheese — 3"x1"x1" — 50 g
2 Slices — 50 g
YOGOURT — 175 g — 3/4 cup

Meat & Alternatives
2-3
SERVINGS PER DAY

1 Serving
Meat, Poultry or Fish — 50-100 g
Fish — 1/3–2/3 Can — 50–100 g
1-2 Eggs
Beans — 125-250 mL — 1/3 cup
TOFU — 100 g
Peanut Butter — 30 mL 2 tbsp

Other Foods

Taste and enjoyment can also come from other foods and beverages that are not part of the 4 food groups. Some of these foods are higher in fat or Calories, so use these foods in moderation.

Acknowledgements

Many thanks to all the staff at the Lazy Gourmet for
their support and help in this project. Also to my family,
Jack, Mira, and Soleil, for putting up with all the chaos!
SUSAN MENDELSON

I would like to acknowledge the help and support of my
husband, Allan Detsky and my sons Michael and Jeffrey who
taught me more about feeding children than any textbook.
I would also like to thank Ryerson Polytechnic University and the
faculty, staff and students of the School of Nutrition, Consumer
and Family Studies for making it possible for me to work on
this book. Elias Chu deserves special mention for typing
the earliest drafts of the project.
RENA MENDELSON

Index

during pregnancy, 33–4
and neural tube defects (NTDs), 33
sources of, 34
food(s):
    requirements for babies, 158–9
    restrictions, 16
    second year, 157, 159–60
formula, about, 147–8
fussing, 148–9

G
genetics, and body shape, 193–4
growth spurts, 190–1

H
healthy diets, choosing, 176–81
heartburn, 39–40
hemoglobin, 30
high blood pressure, and calcium, 27
honey, and babies, 157
hyperactivity, and sugar, 197
hypercarotenemia, 155

I
iodine, need for, 37
iron:
    cookware, 200
    deficiency, 30, 159, 199–200
    and formula-fed babies, 151
    and pregnancy, 30–2
    sources of, 32
    supplements, 31–2
    and vitamin C, 200
isotretinoin, and vitamin A, 38
IUD, and anemia, 18

L
lactose intolerance, 27–8, 201–202
liver, and vitamin A, 31

M
malnutrition, 199
meal patterns, 183–4
meals, timing of, 154
media, and food messages, 203–204
medical check ups, 190
megadoses, vitamin C, 38
met-hemoglobinemia, 155
microwave ovens, 156
milk, 153
    allergies, 201–202
    needs in second year, 160
    see also breastfeeding
mineral supplements, 142
    and babies, 150–1
multivitamin supplements, 37–8
    overdoses of, 198–9
muscles, and calcium, 27

N
nausea, coping with, 25–6
neural tube defects (NTDs), 33
nitrite, in food, 155
nursing mothers:
    need for calcium, 141–2
    and nutrition, 141–3
nutrient(s):
    -dense diet, 24
    and pregnancy, 26–38
    supplements, 17
nutrition, preconceptional, 15–17

O
obesity, and young children, 193
oral contraceptives, and nutritional
    stores, 17–18
osteoporosis, 27
overweight children, and physical activity,
    197

P
pacifiers, 148
peer pressure, and eating, 182
pernicious anemia, 33
physical activity, and body shape, 194–5
'pica', 199
pill, and iron deficiency, 18
prenatal programs, 16
protein:
    for breakfast, 186
    and vegetarians, 36

R
'restaurant syndrome', 182

S
salt, consumption, 38–9
sandwiches, and school lunches, 188–9
saunas, during pregnancy, 43
school lunches, 188–90
scurvy risk, 38
seafood, introducing, 160
self-feeding, 160
serotonin, 197
smoking, effect on birth weight, 20
snacks, 160, 190
    importance of, 187–8
solid foods, readiness for, 151–6
soya formula, 147
spina bifida, and folic acid, 33
sports injuries, 42–3
steam baths, during pregnancy, 43
stress, during pregnancy, 42
sudden infant death syndrome (SIDS), 20
sugar, 195–8
    and hyperactivity, 197
    obesity, 197
    and tooth decay, 196

Index-Recipes

Linguine:
    with black bean sauce, 104
    with spicy tomato and clam sauce, 102
Liver, imitation, 61

M
Mama Rozzie's:
    chicken soup, 169, 235
    green bean casserole, 246
    matzoh balls, 236
Mango(es):
    for babies, 168
    chutney dressing, 83
Matzoh balls, 236
Meat(s), 51, 210–11
    alternatives to, 51, 210–11
    for babies, 169
Menu(s), 212
    for babies, 171
    daily, 52
Meringues, 126
    pavlova, 129
Microwave mushroom and green pea
    risotto, 93
Milk products, 50, 210
Milk shakes, 274
Minestrone soup, 70
Miso:
    sauce, 216
    soup with tofu, 237
Mixes, nuts and bolts, 264
Mozzarella cheese:
    eggplant-tomato gratin, 99
    and onion quesadillas, 107
Muffins:
    banana-walnut, 228
    bran, 221
    raspberry-blueberry cornmeal, 55
Mushroom:
    and green pea risotto, 93
    nut pâté, 63
Mussels, saffron, 66

N
Nachos, 231
New Wave Caesar salad, 81
Nut(s):
    mushroom pâté, 63
    spinach salad with, 83
    vegetarian burgers, 116
Nuts and bolts mix, 264

O
Oatmeal:
    blueberry scones, 227
    cookies, 265
    pancakes, 223
    porridge, 225

Oats, rolled, granola, 57, 226
Onion, and red pepper quesadillas, 107

P
Pancakes, oatmeal, 223
Papaya:
    for babies, 168
    and yogurt soup, 75
Pasta:
    broccoli noodles, 101
    cauliflower, broccoli and cheddar
      kugel, 92
    cheese and tomato kugel, 91
    fettucine lasagna, 250
    linguine
      with black bean sauce, 104
      with clam sauce, 102
    spinach orzo, 94
    sun-dried tomatoes with, 103
    tofu fettucine, 120
    tuna casserole, 253
    tuna salad, 89
Pâté, mushroom nut, 63
Pavlova, 129
Peach(es):
    August soup, 74
    for babies, 168
    berry crisp, 124
    cantaloupe soup, 77
    shortcake, 128
    smoothie, 275
Peanut butter:
    and honey granola bars, 266
    krispies, 268
Peanut sauce, 120, 218, 219, 244
Pea(s):
    and mushroom risotto, 93
    for babies, 166
Pesto:
    sauce, 262
    and vegetable soup, 68
    with Chèvre, 59
Phyllo:
    spinach in, 106
    spinach and tofu in, 118
Pita:
    party pockets, 278
    pizza, 248
    tuna pineapple, 247
Pizza, 260
    dough, 258
      whole wheat, 259
    four-cheese, 263
    pita, 248
    sauce, 261
Polenta, 98
Poppyseed dressing, 79
Pops, frozen, 272–3
Porridge, 225